Mira Bai belonged to the royal family of the Rānās of Mewara and was a staunch devotee of Krishna, worshipping him in the *mādhurya bhāva* of Vaishnavism. In the earlier part of her life she was ill-treated by her brother-in-law who even tried various means to kill her, but Krishna was ever her protector. Fed up, she went away to Merata, her maternal home and from there to Vrindavana and then to Dvaraka, where, according to traditional belief, she merged with the image of Krishna.

Mira's verses have a musical ring and a number of them have been recorded on discs and cassettes. There have been many recensions of her *padas*. This English verse translation of eighty-one of them aims at giving the best of these.

It is hoped that Mira's verses, along with the detailed introduction giving her life and times and her art, will create renewed interest in this renowned saint-poet.

Krishna P. Bahadur was born in 1924 at Allahabad and took his Master's degree in English from the Allahabad University. He served in the Indian Administrative Service in various assignments and retired in 1982 with the rank of a Commissioner.

A prolific writer, Bahadur has authored over fifty books covering various subjects including philosophy, history, biography, sociology, fiction, humour, and juveniles. His writings include the *Wisdom of India Series*, 7 vols., *History of Indian Civilization*, 7 vols., *History of the Indian Freedom Movement*, 5 vols., *Tribes and Cultures of India*, 7 vols., *A Source Book of Indian Philosophy*, and *The Definitive Gita*. He took part in the World Seminar on the *Gita* and contributed to *Major World Writers*.

He is a biographer of various prestigious publications published in USA, Great Britain and Italy, and has received several honorary awards including Vidya Visharada and Vidya Ratnakara. He has published also six translations in the UNESCO Collection of Representative Works.

Mīrā Bāī and Her Padas

Mīrā Bāī
Courtesy: The Gita Press, Gorakhpur

Mīrā Bāī
and
Her Padas

Translated into English verse
with an Introduction by
Krishna P. Bahadur

Munshiram Manoharlal
Publishers Pvt. Ltd.

ISBN 81-215-0786-3
This edition 2002

© 2002, **Bahadur,** Krishna P. (b. 1924)

Printed and published by
Munshiram Manoharlal Publishers Pvt. Ltd.,
Post Box 5715, 54 Rani Jhansi Road,
New Delhi 110 055.

To my beloved daughter
Sandhya
(16 October 1963–17 March 1979)

Yet in these ears, till hearing dies,
   One set slow bell will seem to toll
   The passing of the sweetest soul
That ever look'd with human eyes.
          —Tennyson, *In Memoriam*

Contents

CHAPTER 5

MĪRĀ'S POETICAL ART

CHAPTER 6

THE NATURE OF MĪRĀ'S LOVE

CHAPTER 7

THE SONGS OF MĪRĀ

Preface

Poet and Saint! to thee alone are given
The two most sacred names of earth and heaven.

—Abraham Cowley

Mīrā was a princess of a royal household. In one of her verses (79) she speaks of the *rangamahala,* an apartment in palaces set apart for sensual enjoyments of rulers and kings. But having immersed herself in Krishna-devotion from her very childhood, she had no use for riches or worldly pleasures. She had no guru as many other saints had. Nor did she need to have one, for she was in direct communion with Krishna, whom she conceived as Lover, Husband, Beloved, Lord and Master. But she had reverence for all holy men and sadhus, in whose company she moved in the latter years of her life. She had no reservations about caste, for she spoke of the distinguished low-caste devotee, Ravidāsa, with reverence. She could 'talk with crowds and keep her virtue and walk with kings—nor lose the common touch.'

Disgusted with the lasciviousness of princely living, Mīrā sought refuge with the sadhus. Enumerating the nine ways of devotion, Shri Rama told his low-caste woman devotee, Shabari, that the first and the most significant was the company of the saints—*prathama bhagati santanha kara sangā.*[1] So Mīrā was only following what the scriptures approved. The sadhus were a pious lot, singing the praises of God, and often having *kīrtanas* (community singing and dancing). Imposters were rare, and when Mīrā was faced with any such pretenders to holiness, she knew how to deal with them. There was, for instance, the carnal-minded 'sadhu' who came to her and said that 'it was Krishna's command that he should make love to her!' While another woman might have been aghast, she quietly told him that as it was Krishna's bidding she couldn't refuse. Lying on the bed in the full gaze of the assembled sadhus, she asked him to go ahead with the lovemaking. The wily man hung his head in shame and begged forgiveness, beseeching her to give him the gift of devotion.[2]

In dancing before the image of Krishna in temples, too, Mīrā was only following an old and very exalted tradition. The dance in India is considered to be an act of devotion and is closely associated with mythology and religion. Revered as Nataraja, Shiva is considered to be the lord of the dance, embodying the eternal cycle of creation, preservation and destruction. Krishna is also closely linked with the Indian dance, particularly his sports with Radha and the cowherd girls. Bharat Nāṭyam, widely practised in the Tamil country, specially in Tanjore and Madras, was one of the oldest varieties of classical Indian dances. Among the ancient exponents of this dance were Devadāsīs, who were greatly accomplished women of high status, learned in the classics and writers on philosophical themes. They had their origin in the early ninth to the eleventh centuries when the Chola kings, particularly Rājarāja I built the great temples of that age. Devadāsīs used to fan the deity, carry the sacred lamp and sing and dance before the images of gods when they were carried in a procession. Thus there was nothing wrong in a Krishna-devotee like Mīrā dancing before Krishna's image. She was only carrying on an old and noble tradition. But the members of her family, who had much valour but little understanding, failed like the Moghul nabobs and the British aristocracy, to distinguish between the cheap and vulgar nautch and Mīrā's spiritually charged dances in the temples. Her ecstatic fervour for Krishna and her association with sadhus were anathema to the rulers of Mewāra. Women of royal families were expected to conduct themselves with regal dignity, and here was Mīrā a princess, putting on a band of jingle-bells round her ankles and dancing in public and consorting with half-clad ochre-robed sadhus!

The Rāṇā decided that Mīrā should not be allowed to besmirch the honour of the house of Mewāra, and he tried to get rid of her in various ways—poison, snake-bite and so forth. Even her well-wisher, Ūdā Bāi, her sister-in-law, accused her falsely of adultery in order to discredit her with the Rāṇā. Mīrā bore all this persecution with calm fortitude. Although wronged and ill-treated , she never took offence, for neither 'foes nor loving friends' could hurt her. She laughed away all the attempts made on her life, and if one believes in miracles, Krishna was her Preserver.

She was firm in Krishna-love and opposed all attempts to distract her from it. Her unswerving devotion and complete faith in her

Giradhara, gave her strength. She frankly expressed her defiance in some of her verses. In one of them (22) she says 'What do I care for what people say, or for the honour of the clan? I will dance before Krishna.' And in another (30) 'I will sing Krishna's praises, whether men like it or not. I will follow the path taken by sadhus.' Although historical proof is lacking, it is quite possible that on her husband's early death it was expected that she would immolate herself on his funeral pyre. But she firmly refused to do so, saying that it would be pointless wasting a life which could be spent in the service of Krishna. She defied society, her clan and all those who were out to bridle her. In a way she was among the earliest of Indian women to stand up against male chauvinism. Her intention, however, was not to compromise the modesty of women or to make them shamelessly ultramodern, but she boldly resisted tyranny in any form.

Mīrā's verses depict both spontaneity as well as an instinctive aptness for music, as their lilting melody shows. Proficiency in singing and playing on musical instruments were essential requirements for women of royal families in those times. Each song of hers follows a particular *rāga*. There are seven basic notes in Indian music and five others which are sharps and flats. Various combinations of at least five of these is known as a *rāga*, which is the distinguishing feature of Indian music. There are thousands of *rāgas*, but only fifty are actually used. Mīrā used a large number of these *rāgas* in her *padas*, and so they have infinite richness and variety. At the same time there is no denying that she was a consummate artist too, and polished up her verses to perfection.

Mīrā's devotion for Krishna was single-minded. She saw the entire world as Krishna, and had severed all worldly bonds. The world is really a reflection of one's thoughts. One who has a dirty mind sees only dirt around him. There are those perverted critics of Mīrā who believe she was a licentious woman using Krishna as an excuse for her lasciviousness. Mīrā was young, and doubtlessly a lovely woman. So it was easy for the vulgar-minded to cast such aspersions on her. The kind of devotion in which the devotee loves God in a wife-husband sort of relationship is bound to raise eyebrows, for many a man fails to understand the true nature of this highest form of Vaishnava devotion. It is not unusual for the witless to pillory saints. Was not Joan of Arc taken to be a witch? Mīrā had complete faith in Krishna. She never bothered about philosophical reasoning, though many of her verses are highly contemplative. Love of Krishna was all she sought, and she firmly believed that he would free her from the world of sorrows, for did he not say to Arjuna in the *Bhagavadgītā* (18.66) 'take my refuge alone; I will absolve you from all sins?'

Very few women can be called saints as well as poets. Mīrā was among the handful of persons who were blessed by the vision of God. It is related that while Chaitanya was on his travels he saw a man sitting on the roadside who had a book into which he would occasionally peep and instantly be overcome with intense joy. Chaitanya wished to see what that erudite books was, but was amazed to find all the pages except one, blank. On that one page there was only one word, namely 'Rama'. This was the page the man kept glancing at when he opened the book. On Chaitanya's asking him why he was moved by just that one page, the man said, 'If Rama's name wasn't there, and everything else one can conceive of, was in it, of what use would that book be to me?' So too for Mīrā the whole world was Krishna and nothing else. She expressed her rapturous ardour for him in paeans and rhapsodies. She found God in the only way in which he can be found—through love. As Euripides says,

> 'He who thinks not that Love is a mighty god,
> Higher than all the deities of heaven,
> Is all uncultured; or unversed in beauty,
> Knows not the God that ruleth over man.'
>
> —*Auge, Fragment*, 5

The world is like a modern painting, obscure, disjointed and difficult to decipher; a jigsaw puzzle hard to assemble, or as a Persian writer has observed, a book of which the first and the last pages are missing. In the midst of this topsy-turvydom every man is seeking peace of mind; but the ways are different, and most people discover that the things they have been pursuing, bring them more unrest, tension and worries, than peace. So we turn to the saints to find out that in which contentment lies, as Lord Krishna says in the *Gītā* (4.34)—*upadekṣyanti te jñānam jñāninaḥ tatva-darśinaḥ*: 'those sages who have known the Soul will instruct you', or as Christ says: 'seek and ye shall find; knock and it shall be opened to you' (St. Mathew, 7.7).

While much has been written about the men saints of India such as Shri Ramakrishna, Shankara, Chaitanya and others, information about the women saints is meagre. Of these, perhaps the most prominent was Mīrā. Though she was discouraged from seeking the company of saints, she nevertheless visited them often and listened to their discourses on spiritual matters. She spurned wealth and though oppressed and persecuted by her own family, particularly by her brother-in-law, she persisted in Krishnaism, and remained ever immersed in deep love for Krishna.

Mīrā was a princess of a royal household. In one of her verses (79) she speaks of the *rangamahal,* an apartment in palaces set apart for sensual enjoyments of rulers and kings. But having immersed herself in Krishna-devotion from her very childhood she had no use for riches or worldly pleasures. She had no guru, nor did she need to have one for she was in direct communion with Krishna whom she conceived as Husband, Lover, Lord and Master. However, she revered all holy men and in the latter years of her life she was much in their company. She had no reservations about caste. Nevertheless her family did not at all approve of her *kīrtanas* in the company of sadhus and her dancing in temples.

In the *Śrīmadbhagavadgītā* Lord Krishna says that both the worship of a God with form and of the formless Cosmic Absolute, lead one to the Supreme Being, but of the two the worship of the Absolute is fraught with difficulties and miseries—*avyakta hi gati duḥkham* (*Gītā*, 12.5). Mīrā took the easier way to God which the *Gītā*, too, preferred and worshipped the Lord with the rapture of love and unswerving devotion. She surrendered both mind and heart to Krishna, and all her questionings were drowned in the notes of his celestial pipe.

Mīrā expressed the outpourings of her soul in chaste verses, which had a high lyrical and musical quality, so much so that many of them have become delightful *bhajana* (holy songs) sung by eminent singers and recorded on discs and cassettes. A votary of the Vaishnava *mādhurya bhakti,* she lost herself in the ecstasy of Krishna-devotion. Her acquaintance with music and dancing gave her songs a divine fervour. She saw the entire world as Krishna.

The world of today seems to be engulfed in violence and materialism, and sex and sensuality have hypnotized people. Moral values have been relegated to the back-burner. In India, particularly, the Medusian Gorgon of caste is raising its head, and while male chauvinism is gradually being snuffed out in most developed countries,

here we still find bride-burning and various other atrocities perpe-
trated on women. The study of Mīrā's life provides a corrective to
such despicable trends. She shows how the sword of God-devotion
is enough to slay the Minotaur of lasciviousness.

I am grateful to my publisher for bringing out this book timely
and in an attractive format, despite these difficult times.

KRISHNA P. BAHADUR

Lucknow
30 October 1997

REFERENCES

1. *Rāmacaritmānasa*, Araṇya Kāṇḍa, 34.4-5.
2. The incident is mentioned in the *Bhaktamālā*, 478 as follows:
   viṣayī kuṭila eka bhesa dhari sādhu liyo,
   kiyo yom prasaṅga mom som aṅgasaṅga kījie |
   ājñā mokom daī āpa lāla giridhārī,
   'aho śīśa dhari laī kari bhojana hūm lījiye' |
   asabhani samāja mem bichāye seja boli liyo
   'saka aha kauna kī nisanka rasa bhījie' |
   seta mukha bhayo, viṣai bhāva saba gayo,
   nayo pāyana pai āya 'mokom bhakti dāna dījie' ||

Acknowledgements

The author gratefully acknowledges the assistance of the following commentaries on the *padas* of Mīrā Bāī in this English verse translation.

Chunnilal 'Shesha', *Mīrā Padāvalī*, Prabhat Prakashan, Delhi, 1966.

Padmavati, *Mīrān Vyaktitva aur Kṛtitva,* Hindi Pracharak Sansthan, Varanasi, 1973.

Krishnadeva Sharma, *Mirānbāī Padāvalī,* Regal Book Depot, Delhi, 1972.

Bhagawandasa Tiwari, *Mīrān kā Kāvya,* Sahitya Bhawan, Allahabad, 1971.

The author is indebted to the Gita Press, Gorakhpur for the portrait of Mīrā Bāī.

A Note on the Translation of Poetry

The task of translating poetry is notoriously difficult. It is compounded in the case of the modern idiom which seeks to depart from conventional forms and ordinary syntax.

—Edward W. Poitras

The change in poetic taste which has been going on in the United States and Great Britain for the past three or four decades, and which has now come to the Eastern countries as well, is bound to create problems for the translator, particularly when rendering Hindi verse into English. Mr Leonard Nathan of the Department of Rhetoric, University of California, has made some significant observations on this aspect of the problem.

> Modern Hindi has little linguistic similarity to English or to any other Western language, though like German, it locates its verbs at the end of the clauses. While Hindi is a member of the Indo-European family, it shares characteristics with other linguistic families of the Indian subcontinent, for instance, Dravidian, as in its use of the preposition. Where English speakers would say: "by the gate", the Hindi speaker says: "gate by". This characteristic, along with innumerable others, makes the job of translation into English a pursuit of equivalences where few exist. The difficulties are made more acute because Hindi prosody accentuates differences already inherent in the two languages. For instance, Hindi verse very often has, at least to the Western ear, a strong trochaic beat, a fact which automatically disqualifies it as modern by our standards that declare any strongly stressed metre, even the common iambic, to be poetic affectation.*

The task of the translator of much of Hindi verse, modern and even more so not so modern, including the various dialects in which it is spoken and written, is to bridge the gap between the old con-

---

Poems by Agyeya, translation by S.H. Vatsyayana and Leonard Nathan (A Note on the Translation).

ventional style, which seems to be popular in India, and the modern taste for 'heavily colloquial and deliberately idiosyncratic verse'. I have thought it best to make a sort of compromise between the two. The result is verse without rhyme or metre, but not deliberately idiosyncratic or heavily colloquial. Such verse would also ensure that the sense of the original is not lost by enslavement to rhyme and metre. Of course in trying to stretch out to both the worlds, the translation might reach neither. But that is a risk one has to take.

A Note on the Transliteration of the Verses

Diacritical marks have invariably been given in the section of the book containing the *padas* (verses) of Mīrā, but in the narrative part they have been sparingly used so as to make the reading easy. Words like 'karma', 'nirvana', 'avatar' and so forth, which are now part of the English language, have not been italicized.

The letter 'o' (which bears no diacritical mark) is to be pronounced as *o* in 'm*o*re' (not as in 'lion'). The *ṛ* may be pronounced as 'r' but with the tip of the tongue higher up on the upper palate and brushing it with a downward motion. The *ṁ* nasalizes and lengthens the preceding vowel as *n* in bo*n* (French). The *ch* sound is also not found in English. It is pronounced with the tip of the tongue placed higher against the upper palate than in uttering the *c* sound.

The cerebrals *(ṭ, ṭh, ḍ, ḍh, ṇ)* are pronounced with the tongue retroflected. The dentals *(t, th, dh, n)* are pronounced with the tongue against the back of the upper front teeth.

Other marks are explained as follows:

a as *u* in c*u*t	*ṅ* as *n* in wi*n*g
ā as *a* in f*a*ther	*ś* and *ṣ* as *s* in *s*ugar
i as *i* in s*i*t	*g* as *g* in *g*oad
ī as *i* in mach*i*ne	*ṭ* as *t* in *t*ongue
u as *u* in p*u*t	*t, d, n,* are dentals
ū as *u* in r*u*le	*ḍ* as *d* in *d*ent
ṛ as *ri* in r*i*ver	*c* as *ch* in *ch*urch
e as *ay* in m*ay*	

Other letters may be pronounced as they are in English. The letter *n* on which a curved mark has been put—*ñ* is to be pronounced as *ñ* in 'Señor' (Spanish).

I sought him in the Cosmic Absolute
I heard his deeds sung in the Purāṇas
The Vedas made my longing fourfold,
But I could never know his nature or his form.

I searched and searched, but I could find him nowhere,
Nor could anyone tell me where he could be found:
Weary, and filled with despair,
When I lost all hope,
Lo! I saw him in a faraway alcove
Pressing Rādhā's feet with loving care.[*]

—Rasakhān

1

Mīrā's Times

The first half of the sixteenth century in the history of India and along with it that of Rajasthan, the state of Mīrā's ancestors, was one of uncertainty and turmoil. Babur, the first of the Moghuls, had begun to cast his covetous gaze on India. Just about the time Mīrā was born, the Turk was attacking Samarquand (1497 and 1503), in a bid to get a foothold on India. He made two attempts but failed. However, he was a tenacious man, and finally managed to establish the foundation of the Moghul rule in India. He was followed by Humayun, who became king in January 1531 (just two years before Mīrā had left Mewāra for Meratā). Humayun's period was one of internecine struggles between him and the Afghan upstart Sher Shah Sur, grandson of a petty horse-dealer. Sher Shah was able to oust Humayun, and he and his successors continued to rule till Akbar was able to ascend the throne on 14 February 1556 (ten years after Mīrā's death). Thus the period in which Mīrā spent the formative years of her life extends from the time of Babur's establishment of the Moghul rule to about the end of the reign of Sher Shah Sur (AD 1544).

When the Moslem invasion came, there was complete unpreparedness on the part of the Hindus, who had neglected paying attention to defence and were busy building fabulous temples, most of which were ransacked by the invaders. Though they did not lack courage, battles are won by superiority of arms and skilled manoeuvres in both of which the Hindus were wanting. Besides, the Rajputs who were the most intrepid among warriors, were fighting among themselves and even siding with the Moghuls. This made them easy prey. For example, Sisodiā had differences with his Rājmātā, Hansā Bāī, and to settle scores with her he allied himself with Bahadur Shah. It was because the great Hindu kingdoms—Orissa and

Rajasthan in the north and Vijayanagara in the south, and the Rajputs under Rāṇā Sāṅgā—were all engaged in war with one another, that Babur's task of establishing his suzerainty, was made easy. Rāṇā Sāṅgā even toyed with an arrangement with Babur to crush Ibrahim Lodhi, the Delhi sultan. It was as the Italian traveller, Niccolao Manucci, noticed '... the Hindus are up to this day (in Akbar's times) more numerous than the Mohammedans. But they can do nothing against the Moghuls, for from old time it has been the fashion of Rajputs to dispute among themselves. If they were only of one mind they would be able to thrust out every other tribe and race.'[1] Rajput valour was displayed when defeat was certain. It was then that, wearing yellow robes and considering themselves already as dead, they charged the Moghul forces as the legendary Light Brigade 'into the jaws of Death'. For the Moslems however every war against the infidels was a holy war, a *jihād* as they called it. This gave their fighting a ferocity which the Rajputs could never match. When Babur was pitched against the forces of Rāṇā Sāṅgā, he boosted the morale of his troops by reminding them that they were not engaged in a war but in a *jihād*. In his *farmān* of victory which he issued afterwards he quoted the *Quranic* text 'Whoever engages in a holy war, of a truth fights for his own soul—engage in war with the heathen and the impious.'[2]

The constant clan rivalries, internal dissensions, feuds and intrigues of the rulers of Mewāra, must doubtless have been an irritant to Mīrā, and a hindrance in her quest of Krishna (Kṛṣṇa)-devotion. Although the main reason for her leaving Mewāra was the animosity of Vikramājīta, her brother-in-law, this too must have been a contributory factor. Her father-in-law Rāṇā Sāṅgā, had been killed in the war with Babur, and with the death of her husband, too, the ties with her in-laws were finally severed.

The coming of the Moslem invaders also caused a lot of misery and destruction. Wars were often followed by pillages and plunder, for the booty so got was a kind of reward to the victorious soldiers for their pains—kings and chieftains too carrying away a large part of it. There were bloody massacres and *qatl-i-'āms* in which the blood of infidels freely flowed. After Humayun had taken Mandu from Bahadur Shah, he ordered a massacre of the people of that place, and so great was the bloodshed that 'the lanes and the bazaars of Mandu ran red with blood.'[3] Under his orders the town of Cambay was sacked for three days. About Sher Shah Sur, Abbas Khan records in *Tārīkh-i-Sher Shāhī* that when his nobles suggested to him a Deccan campaign, the emperor said, 'Until I have cleansed the country of the existing contamination of the unbelievers I will not go into any other country.' The Moslem invaders treated even Hindu women with the utmost contempt. When Sher Shah stormed Raisen, a fort held by a Hindu chief, Purana Malla, the Rajputs slew their own women to preserve their honour. However, one of his daughters and three sons of his elder brother, somehow fell in their hands. Sher Shah gave the princess to an itinerant Moslem minstrel *(bāzīgarān)* to make her dance in the bazaars, and got the boys castrated that 'the race of the oppressor might not increase.'[4] But when he captured Moslem women after Humayun's defeat at Chausa, all of them, even the slave-girls, were treated with honour, Sher Shah providing the families of the Moghuls with carriages and their necessary expenses.'[5] Such was the racial discrimination between the daughter of a Hindu ruler and even a Moslem slave-girl!

We have mentioned specifically Humayun and Sher Shah as they reigned in Mīrā's period of time. But it was the same with almost all Moslem rulers, even Akbar, who is hailed as being broadminded. In fact one should say *especially* Akbar, for when three hundred Rajput women flung themselves into the flames in a mass-immolation *(jauhar)* after the fall of Bednor, frustrated perhaps because he had not been able to obtain any of the princesses for his harem, he ordered a general massacre which went on for three days. Apart from 8,000 combatants, 30,000 peasants who were mere servants, were killed. The temples and towers were razed to the ground. The number of those slaughtered was so great that their sacred threads alone weighted about seventy-five maunds (six thousand pounds).[6] Akbar left the soulless burning city with the corpses rotting on the streets, a monument to his rage and frustration, after handing it to Asaf Khan.

Mewāra, which had to bear the brunt of the Moslem onslaught, had a fascinating history. Now called Rajasthan, and in the pre-Mohammedan days, Rajputana, it was ruled in the ancient period by a few prominent tribal dynasties, of which the earliest were the Chalukyas and the Rashtrakutas. Thereafter power passed into the hands of the Rathors of Kanuaj, the Chauhans of Ajmer, the Solankis of Anhilwara, the Gahilots or Sisodiyas of Mewāra and the Kachhwahas of Jaipur.

The most prominent principality of Mewāra was Guhila. In the seventh century the people of this clan of Rajputs established themselves here. 'Alā-ud-dīn organized an expedition against the Guhila Rajputs which culminated in the fall of the fort of Chittor. It is said that this was partly because of his infatuation for Padminī, the attractive wife of Rāṇā Ratan Singh. Tod relates in his *Annals* how, to escape the lascivious monarch, Padminī perished in a massive *jauhar* along with several thousand women and royal princesses, while the valorous Rajputs, outnumbered, fought with 'Alā-ud-dīn's huge army and died to a man. According to Amir Khusrau, who was an eye-witness, 30,000 Rajputs were killed in one day. Hammir recovered Chittor from the Moslems. He was, as Tod says 'one of the wisest and most gallant of Mewāṛa's princes.' The next great ruler was Rāṇā Kumbha, who was not only a valiant warrior but also a poet and a patron of music and literature. Unfortunately he was cruelly assassinated by his own son, Udaya Karan (about AD 1469). After a dispute about succession, Rāṇā Sāṅgā became ruler in 1509, and in the words of Tod, 'with this prince Mewāṛa reached the summit of her prosperity.' He fought Babur but was defeated at the memorable battle of Khanua (1527) and died soon after. Khanua destroyed the prospect of replacing the Delhi sultanate with a Rajput empire, and perpetuated the rule of Moslems in India.

Mīrā must have learnt about the devastation caused by the Moghul invaders and their bigotry, even though she was not in the midst of it. But even more distressing must have been the petty animosities and intrigues among the Rāṇās of Mewāṛa themselves, who, even when faced by external danger were constantly fighting one another. After the dastardly assassination of Kumbha by Udaya Karan, Udaya's brother was chosen as ruler. But Udaya opposed him, even seeking the support of Sultan Ghayas-ud-dīn. What was more degrading was that in order to get the Sultan's assistance, he bartered his own daughter to him in marriage. Thus Rajput princesses, who traditionally immolated themselves to protect their honour, were given away as concubines to swell Moslem harems. Such was the tainted fire of overvaulting ambition—a fire shorn of the purity of the *jauhars*. The three sons of Rayamala—Prithiviraja, Jayamala and Sangram Singh—were continually fighting among themselves for the crown, with the result that in the ensuing internecine warfare Sangram Singh lost one eye. Jayamala wished to marry the daughter of Solanki Rao Suratana. But the Rao did not consent, and as a consequence war broke out between them. Rāṇā

Rayamala's daughter, Anandabai was married to Rao Jayamala of Sirohi. As he was ill-treating her, Prithiviraja, who was her brother, admonished him. Feeling insulted by this, the Rao of Sirohi poisoned Prithiviraja. We have related these incidents to show the ferocity of the clan rivalries and domestic feuds among the Rajputs, which made them powerless to oppose the Moslem invaders.

SOCIETY

Caste has been the curse of the Hindu social system ever since the Paurāṇika age. There was no let up in this pernicious evil, except that the compartments did not remain as watertight as before. With the mass destruction of temples brahmins lost their priestly avocation and many took up trade, or became warriors. Sudras were in some cases rulers and fighters. But such isolated instances could not dent the steel frame of the Hindu caste system. The oppression of the Sudras was its worst aspect, and created bitterness which became difficult to eradicate. The Rajputs emerged as the ruling families of northern India. The Moslem nobility remained confined to the main cities, for the villages of the countryside never attracted them, except for extracting revenue. A feature of the ingress of the Moslems was the growth of slavery. Moslem conquerors were eager to carry away Hindu girls as slaves. They made no distinction between a common girl and one of a high family. Hindu princesses were forced into harems to satiate the lust of Moslem kings and commanders. Quite often a present was made of them to foreign potentates. Mohammed bin Tughluq sent the Chinese emperor 'one hundred men as slaves and one hundred slave songstresses dancers from among the Indian infidels.'

A significant feature of the age was the licentiousness of high society. Both Hindu rulers and Moslem nabobs were alike in this, sipping wine in wine-glasses and casting glances of lascivious admiration, as dancing-girls whirled in tantalizing gyrations. Although the Islamic creed prohibited drinking, most Moslem rulers drank. Abundance of wealth captured as spoils of war or loot corrupted morals, and prostitutes, nautch-girls and concubines figured largely in Moslem life. Manucci says, 'all Mohammedans are very fond of women, who are their principal relaxation and almost their only pleasure.'[7] Careri too noticed the wantonness of Moslem living. 'They spend all that have in luxury, keeping a vast number of servants, but above all of concubines. These being many, every one of them strives to be beloved above the rest, using all manner of allurements, perfumes and sweet ointments. Sometimes to heighten their master's lusts, they give him compositions of pearls, gold, opium and amber; or else much wine, that he may require company in bed. Then some drive away the flies, others rub his hands and feet, other dance, others play on music and others do other things.'[8] Gambling, cheating and even homosexuality, were other vices which the Moslems brought. Manucci mentions 'wretched pretenders to holiness who satisfy their lust and avarice.'[9] The Hindu chieftains were only a shade better. They kept many wives and often mistresses, and in imitation of their Moslem counterparts, slave-girls too. Women had a bad deal and were often given in marriage without their consent. In fact marriage alliances were more or less for cementing relations between royal families. Besides Hindu women had little marital freedom. Divorce was unknown, and many wives, as for example Bahiṇā who was thrashed by her husband and Mīrā who was tortured by her brother-in-law, were victims of male oppression and brutality. The aristocracy, both Hindu and Moslem, had become corrupt beyond measure. Not content with their mistresses and slaves, royal rulers and princes would send their emissaries to the countryside in distant villages to seek out young and good looking virgins to satiate the ever-raging fire of their lust. Innocent girls were thus made victims on the altar of lasciviousness of potentates.

The obnoxious Hindu practice of suttee was in existence before the coming of the Moslems, but their advent exacerbated it because they invariably carried away Hindu women after a conquest and dishonoured them. Most often suttee was not voluntary. The life of a Hindu widow was an extremely miserable one. She could dress only in a plain borderless sari and was deprived of all ornaments. She could not in any way adorn herself. A widow was considered to be inauspicious and her company was shunned. She could not take part in many of the Hindu festivals. Thus her existence was a kind of life-in-death. If a woman chose to immolate herself on her husband's funeral pyre in these circumstances, it can't be said she did so voluntarily. It was in fact as though the entire Hindu society conspired to push her into the flames, while the onlookers gazed at this 'heroic' offering in smug satisfaction which was a combination of religious frenzy and sadistic glee. In the case of immolation to save dishonour, the motive was quite different and the act praiseworthy, for in that case death was to escape being raped by lusty Moslem soldiers, and for the princesses a miserable life as slave-girls or concubines in Moslem harems. Many of the suttees and *jauhars* carried out in Mīrā's troubled times were of this nature.

A new element introduced in Hindu society, following the Moslem rule, was the veil (purdah). So far the veil (called *ghūṁghaṭa*) was purely a domestic custom followed by newlyweds and confined to the family. Partly in imitation of the rulers and partly to protect themselves, Hindu women, particularly of the higher classes, adopted the veil in society too. The middle-class Hindu women, however, merely covered their heads with a shawl, and those of the lower classes often discarded it altogether, women water-carriers moving about freely without purdah.

Despite all these restraints, women excelled in learning and often took an active part in affairs of state. Mīrā Bāī wrote devotional songs. Ramabhadramba, Madhuravani and Tirumalambha distinguished themselves in Sanskrit poetry. In administration there were Rani Karmavati and the Maratha queen Tanabai Mohite. Vikramājīta's mother, Hare Rani looked after the kingdom of Chittor during the regency of her son and also fought wars when the occasion arose. Thus the role of women often crossed the confines of hearth and home.

RELIGIOUS TRENDS

At the end of the period of Hindu rule Buddhism became prominent. Soon, however, it was replaced by the Brahmanical religion. The Krishna cult developed in northern India. The *Bhāgavata Purāṇa* had narrated various episodes in Krishna's life. But now the love of Rādhā and Krishna began to be particularly emphasized. A highly erotic element was added by works such as the *Gīta-govinda* of Jayadeva and the *Brahmavaivarta Purāṇa*.

In the south the Vaishnava religion prevailed in a more elevated form. A new school was founded by Acharya Nathamuni which produced saint-philosophers like Yamunacharya and his celebrated disciple Ramanuja. Another devotional school was that of the Āḷvārs, to which Ramanuja was inclined in his later years. After Ramanuja's death in 1137, the Vaishnavas were plagued by a schism which split them into two groups. Ramanuja had sponsored the scriptures written in Sanskrit as well as those in Tamil. After him the Sanskrit enthusiasts, known as the Vaḍakalais believed the Vedas, Upaniṣads and the *Gītā* to be superior, while the Tamil group, the Teṅkalais confined sanctity to the Tamil Prabandhas. The Teṅkalais thought the low-castes could study the scriptures and recite the sacred *mantras*, while the Vaḍakalais believed they couldn't. Another fundamental difference between them was that the Vaḍakalais gave importance to effort, while the Teṅkalais believed in God's grace. According to the former school it is only when one strives for emancipation and makes a sincere effort towards it, he can reach the goal. This, however is only the first step. After making the effort the devotee realizes that the effort by itself is of no avail. The feeling of helplessness makes him turn to God, and he surrenders himself completely to him. According to the Teṅkalais no such effort is needed. God's love is spontaneous and he has the power of condoning all sins. All the evils of the person whom he favours are destroyed. Thus the Teṅkalais believed in the supremacy of God's grace.

The most prominent among religious saints of the 15th–16th centuries was Ramananda who emphasized love and worship of God. He was no stickler for caste and admitted to his fold people of the low-caste also. Among his disciples there was a weaver, a barber and a cobbler. Ravidasa, Kabir, Sena, Dhanna, Pipa, Sukhananda, Surasurananda and others were of Ramananda's school. Tulsidasa was greatly influenced by Kabir, and so was the great saint and mystic Dādū (b. AD 1544). All these disciples were sages of high understanding. Kabir was the son of a Mohammedan weaver. He believed in simple living but not in an idle existence. He wanted everyone to be industrious and to earn his living, but he was against the hoarding of wealth. He made no distinctions between castes and religions, putting his trust in truth and love. The brahmins were against him but nonetheless his spiritual teachings attracted some of them and they became his disciples. Two of these were Tatvaji and Jivaji, who by acknowledging him as their guru incurred the wrath of their fellow-brahmins. They were ostracized and no one would take their children in marriage. One of them had a son and the other a daughter. They went to Kabir for advice. He said it was no problem at all, for the girl and the boy could marry each other.[10] Ravidasa, a cobbler by birth, worshipped the One Infinite Being whom he considered as beyond all sects without beginning or end. He believed that God resides in the hearts of all creatures. He cannot be reached by rites and ceremonies, but only through inner devotion and love. As Krishna says in the *Bhagavadgītā*, 'I cannot be seen or known by the study of the Vedas, or by the practice of austerities, or by the giving of charity, or by carrying out sacrifices. I can be realized only through single-minded devotion.'[11] Mīrā's devotion, too, was of this kind. She had to suffer a lot of persecution, sadly from her own family members, who sometimes even branded her as a licentious woman under the misconception that love could be only for human beings, and thinking that her Giradhara (Krishna) was some lover who secretly visited her. But she did not care for such slander and was courageous enough to stand up and face it. Her sole support was Krishna, her heart's lord and her companion not only in her lifetime but in past lives too—*puraba janama kā sāthī*. In her heart were both the disease and the doctor, suffering and its reliever, the wounds and the balm.[12] She was wholly engrossed in Krishna and her love was expressed in a very intimate manner. 'He has gone away somewhere without telling me', she says, 'maybe to someone else's house. He came, but went away after going round my courtyard; and when he did come to me, alas! I was asleep. I kept waiting for him night and day. But what is the use of meeting him? He speaks sweetly, but refuses to give me his love. O Yogi Lover, do not go away, do not go, do not go! I prostrate myself at your feet.'

In her sufferings and hardships, in the calumnies and scandals heaped on her, in unjust castigation which could not distinguish between human and divine love, in suffering indignities because she was a woman; Mīrā portrayed the general harshness and apathy which assailed all womankind. She had to bear rough treatment and hear bitter words, often without any cause, as when her family priest got annoyed with her merely because she wanted him to sing a particular hymn before the idol in the temple. He got so worked up by this innocent request that he burst out saying, 'O accursed widow! which song is this? ... I will not see your face even again.'[13] This must have hurt her, for she always spoke gently, even as she depicted her Beloved Lord in her songs—*mīṭho thāre baina* and *mīṭho thāre bola*. Mīrā's love for Krishna was too subtle and elevated to be understood by those with coarse minds. It was a kind of worship, for she had given her mind and her heart to her Giradhara.

Some writers are of the view that the Bhakti cult of India was the consequence of the impact of Sufism.[14] In fact the possibility could be the other way about. Nonetheless Sufism has ideas often similar to the devotional creed of Vaishnavism. Yahya, son of Ma'az says: 'A Sufi gives up all worldly pleasures. He does not desire even paradise. He only desires union with his Beloved. He cannot see anything other than God.' Bayazid says, 'There's nothing apart from God. The cup, the wine and the drinker of wine are one and the same.' Ahmad, a native of Balkh (Afghanistan) believed 'God can be seen. Surely they are blind who cannot see him.' There is no positive evidence to show that Mīrā was influenced by the Sufis, but it could be that among the holy men whose company she kept, there were some Sufi saints too.

REFERENCES

1. *Storia do Mogor*, trans., William Irvine, vol. 1.
2. *Memoirs of Babur*, trans., Leyden and Erskine, p. 354.
3. *History and Culture of the Indian People*, ed., R.C. Majumdar, vol. VII, p. 43.
4. Abbas Khan, *Tārīkh-i-Sher Shāhī*.
5. Ibid.
6. *The Cambridge History of India*, vol. 4, p. 99.
7. Manucci, *Storia do Mogor*, vol. 2, p. 342.
8. Careri, *A Voyage Round the World*, part III, p. 251.
9. Manucci, op. cit., vol. 2, pp. 13-14.
10. *Bhaktamālā*, 313: *Kānā-kānī bhaī, dvija jāti jāti gaī | pāmti nyārī kari daī, koū beṭī nahiṁ leta haiṁ | calyo eka kāśī jahāṁ basata kabīr dhīra | jaya kahī pīra, jaba pūchyo kauna heta hai | doū tuma bhai karau āpu meṁ sagaī | hoya bhakti sarasāī, na dharaī cita ceta hai | āya vahai kari, parī jñāti kharabharī | kahaiṁ kahā ura dharī, kachu mati hūeg aceta hai ||*
11. *Bhagavadgītā*, 11.43–44.
12. *Jā ghaṭa birahā soī lakhi hai, kaī koī harijana mānai hoṁ | rogī antara vaida basata hai, vaida hī okhada jānai ho ||*
13. *Are ḍārī rāṇa yaha kauna ko pada hai... āje te tero muṁharau kabahuṁ na dekhūṁgau |* (*Mīrābāī kī Padāvalī*)
14. Yusuf Husain, *Glimpses of Medieval Indian Culture*, p. 13.

2

Life

Mīrā fearlessly sang of love,
Unmindful of the wicked men who wanted her death.
She drank unflinchingly the poison sent to her, as though
   it was nectar.
She did not care for what people said
And boldly sounded the drum of Krishna-devotion.*

—*Bhaktamālā*

(*niramkuśa niḍara ati rasika jasa rasanā gāyau* |
duṣṭani doṣa vicāri mṛtyu kau uddima kiyau |
bāra na bāṁke bhayau, garala amṛta jyauṁ piyau |
bhakti nisāna bajāya ke kāhū te nā lajī |
loka laja taji mīrā giradhara bhajī ||)

DATE AND PLACE OF BIRTH

As in the case of other saints there is no direct evidence about Mīrā's date of birth. A letter of Purohitji to Ojha of 9 September 1938 candidly admits 'the exact dates of Mīrā's birth and death are not known.'[1] Other scholars have assigned various dates: Dholerava Bhat 1505–6; Kunwar Sukhvira Singh Gahlot 1497–98; R.S. Devashri, barrister, Mewāṛa 1499–1500; Munshi Deviprasada 1503–4; Thakur Chatura Singh Rathora 1457–58; Grierson 1420; Jhaveri 1403 and Keay 1470.[2] Of these Devashri's view is perhaps the most acceptable as he was a barrister in Mewāṛa and would be knowing about Mīrā's family firsthand.

There is also considerable difference of opinion about Mīrā's place of birth. Some scholars are of the view that she was born in Meṛatā village, others put it at Chokari, and yet others at Kuraki. According to Kalyanamala Shekhavat it was village Bajauli and

---

*Author's translation.

Kuraki was the place where she lived for some time after her birth.[3] Dr Parashurama Chaturvedi is of the firm opinion that Mīrā was born in Kuraki village.[4]

NAME

There is also difference of opinion in regard to Mīrā's name. Some writers believe it was only a nickname or family name and Bāī was added to it as her surname. Others believe that Mīrā itself was her surname and her first name (Christian name) was some other. Dr Barthaval says, ' "Mīrā" was not a name at all and it just means "The wife of Ishvara (God)" '.[5] Purohit Harinarayana comes out with the fantastic view that Shahsufi of Ajmere was the person who inspired the name 'Mīrā', and she was named after him. This could not at all be possible, for the Shah was considered to be an enemy of the Rajputs and was later slain by them.[6] How could the name of a woman of the family of Rāṇās be ever associated with a foe? There are other views, equally fantastic. One is that Meratā signifies Mīratā, i.e., Mīrā + tā, and since water is plentiful there as the place is full of tanks, Mīrā was named so because of that. Another suggestion is that her name was not Mīrā but Mīraṁ or Mīrān.[7] This is only hair-splitting, for in reality both are the same. However, it seems to be popular with some scholars, as for example Dr Padmavati and Dr Bhagawandasa Tewari. In this book we have accepted Mīrā as the saint-poet's name.

There is also no definite evidence of the names of Mīrā's father and mother. However, the views of various scholars are as follows.

Regarding Her Father
1. According to the commentary of Priyadasa on *Bhaktamālā*, *Rasa-prabīdhihī*, her parents remained alive for long, but their names are not mentioned.[8]
2. Colonel Tod has given the name of Mīrā's father as Rao Duda and at other places as Ratna Singh, who was the Rao's son.[9]
3. In the *Vīra-vinoda* the various names of Mīrā's father are given as Ratna Singh the fifth son of Rao Duda, another Ratna Singh the younger brother of Rao Birandeva, and thirdly, Birandeva himself.
4. In the records of Mewāṛa collected by Munshi Deviprasada, Mīrā is said to be the daughter of Rao Duda, or of Rathora Rao Ratna Singh, the grandson of Rao Duda.

5. According to Gaurishankar H. Ojha, Ratna Singh was the fourth son of Rao Duda, not the fifth, as the *Vīra-vinoda* says.

Thus while various views have been advanced by different scholars, there is no definite testimony about the name of Mīra's father. Nonetheless it seems most of the sources point to Ratna Singh, and he was the son of Rao Duda—which son, the second, fourth, or fifth, is neither clear, nor is it of any consequence.

Mīrā's Mother

Equally vague is the testimony about Mīrā's mother. According to Vidyananda Sharma her mother was Kusuma Kunwar.[10] Purohitji is of the view that Mīrā was the daughter of Virakumari.[11] Some scholars think that her mother died early, others that she lived long. However, Sharma's view seems to be the most acceptable one.

Considering the various views of scholars and commentators, it seems most probable that Mīrā was born in AD 1500 in the village of Kuraki, her parents were Ratna Singh and Kusuma Kunwar, and her husband Raja Bhoja. She died in AD 1546 when she was forty-six years old.

THE EARLY YEARS

Rao Duda was a staunch Vaishnava and so Mīrā was brought up in an atmosphere of devotion, which was later to become her sole quest and objective. The probability is that Mīrā's mother died early, though according to some writers both her parents were long-lived.[12] It is certain, however, that after her mother's death it was Rao Duda who brought her up. Because of this she imbibed early the Vaishnava spirit of devotion and worship, waving the sacred lamp before the image of Krishna, making the sacred food-offering, dressing up the idol and prostrating herself before the Lord. We know almost nothing about her early education, but she must have acquired adequate knowledge of several dialects like Brajabhasha, Rajasthani and the other local ones. It seems she had also learnt Sanskrit under the guidance of Rao Duda.[13]

When Mīrā was yet in her teens she was married, for the custom of early marriages was then prevalent. As with her birth and parentage, considerable vagueness exists about the name of her husband and the date of her marriage. J.N. Farquhar says that Mīrā Bāī, a princess of the house of Meratā in Jodhpur 'became the wife of the heir apparent to the Mewāra throne, but he died before the accession of his father (the great Kumbha Rāṇa, AD 1469). Left a widow and rather ungenerously treated by her brother-in-law who had succeeded to the throne, she left Chittor and became the disciple of Raidasa Ramanandi, and then a devotee of Krishna.'[14] *The Cultural Heritage of India* has the following account:

> Mīrābāī was the daughter of Raja Ratna Singh and the daughter-in-law of Raja Sanghaji. Her nine or ten years of domestic life with her husband Raja Bhoja were years of quiet and unperturbed happiness, but her troubles began when she became a widow. Driven by the unjust treatment of her brother-in-law, she sought refuge in her father's home, but finally gave up the world altogether and adopted the life of an ascetic. The story goes that Mīrā, a worshipper of Girdharilal at first, was initiated by Ravidasa into the worship of the One and the infinite. But though she might have been influenced by the ideals of Ravidasa, it is very difficult to associate them chronologically.[15]

According to J.C. Oman, Mīrā was married to the Raja of Udaipur.[16] Colonel Tod in his *Annals* says that Mīrā was the wife of the Raja of Kumbha. G.A. Grierson also supports this view: 'This remarkable woman ... was married to Rāṇā Kumbha Karan, son of Mocal Deb of Chittor. Her husband was killed by his son, Udai Rāṇā.'[17]

These, however, are only casual references. A full account occurs earliest in the commentary on the *Bhaktamālā*. According to this Mīrā was married to some Rāṇā. But when she came to her new home, her cruel mother-in-law hated her and complained about her to her son. The Rāṇā sided with his mother and got Mīrā confined in a secluded apartment in the palace and put guards round it. Thus husband and wife virtually lived separate and the guards kept conveying the welfare of one to the other. In his *Padaprasaṅga-mālā* Nagaridasa says that Mīrā was married to the younger brother of the Rāṇā, who died soon after the marriage. The Rāṇā asked Mīrā to immolate herself on the funeral pyre of her husband according to the practice of suttee prevalent, but she was deep in devotion to the Lord Hari and already away from all worldliness. So she refused to burn herself alive (for that would defeat God's purpose in conferring on her the gift of life). Instead, she went to Vrindavana and from there to Dvaraka (places associated with Krishna). However, the verses alleged to be Mīrā's, on which Nagaridasa, commentator of the *Bhaktamālā,* relies, are not available, and so the account of her marriage lacks evidence.

There are other conflicting views about this. Munshi Deviprasada believes she was married to Bhojaraja, son of Mahārāṇā Sāṅgā but the marriage did not last long for Bhojaraja died young. Shambhuprasada Bahuguna considers her husband to be Rāṇā Rāyemala, son of Rāṇā Kumbha. Nor is there any reliable evidence of Mīrā's widowhood. One view is that her marriage lasted long, but according to another her husband died early, a few years after marriage. As we have said, it seems most probable that her husband was Raja Bhoja.

There are many legends narrated about Mīrā's early life. It is said that once while she was yet a child, a sadhu came to her house. He had with him a very lovely image of Krishna. The girl was charmed with it and liked to possess it. She beseeched him to give it to her, but he wouldn't listen. When he had gone, Mīrā was so overcome with disappointment that she pined with sorrow and wasted away. Meanwhile the sadhu had a vision in which he heard Lord Hari say, 'Go and give this idol to Mīrā'. Amazed, the sadhu hastened and handed it to her. Mīrā rejoiced and recovered her health. Another incident widely related is that once a marriage-party came to Mīrā's village. When she saw it the girl innocently asked her mother, 'Mother, who is *my* husband?' 'Your husband' her mother said, 'is that Giradharalal whose image is ever in your hands.' From that moment Mīrā considered herself to be the beloved of Lord Hari. She has expressed this in many of her verses.[18] There is another story told of a brahmin who came to Rāṇā Kumbha. The Rāṇā was so pleased with him that he told him to ask for any boon he desired. The brahmin asked for the hand of the Rāṇā's youngest wife. The Rāṇā was in a fix. He said, 'All right, you go to the different palace apartments, and in whichever you do not find me, you may take that queen as your wife.' The brahmin went to every apartment, but was amazed to find the Rāṇā in each one of them.

We see therefore that Mīrā's life is shrouded in mystery. There are views and views but little historical evidence to go by. To add to this there are a number of legends about her, which may be given credence to or rejected as one wishes. We have to build a picture which emerges from these accounts, for with saints the dividing line between the credible and the incredible is very thin indeed.

After the death of her father, Ratna Singh, Mīrā was left sorrow-ful and desolate, and she turned to devotion to Krishna, the seed of which had already been sown in her early years. She loved to move in the company of holy men and, breaking the barrier of seclusion, which in those days obliged women to be completely confined to their homes, she attended religious gatherings and listened to the discourses of sadhus. She would often wear ankle-bells and dance before the idol of Krishna in temples, clapping her hands in tune.[19]

Rāṇā Sāṅgā, Mīrā's father-in-law, who was away fighting the Moghul invader Babur, was killed in one of the battles. His death finally severed Mīrā's connection with her husband's family. After his death her brother-in-law Vikramajita, ascended the throne of Mewāra. His advent began a chapter of cruel oppression for Mīrā. He was incensed against her because he resented her moving about with sadhus and publicly dancing before the Krishna-idol in tem-ples. He considered such conduct derogatory for a woman of the royal household. So great was his anger that he tried the basest of means to kill the innocent woman. On one occasion he sent her a cup of poison ordering her to drink it. Mīrā drained it off, but it had no effect on her: 'The Rāṇā sent me a cup of poison, which I drank, thinking it to be nectar.'[20] How could that person come to harm whose protector was the Lord himself! According to legend it was Krishna who took upon himself the evil effect of the poison, leaving Mīrā unharmed. It is said that the idol of Krishna turned blue as soon as Mīrā had emptied the cup. This could be dismissed as mere make-believe. However there is mention of the incident in *Mahakamem Tavārīkh Mewāra*, though it seems it is not clear at whose instance the poison was given.[21] The *Mahakamem Tavārīkha Mewāra* mentions Mīrā's tormentor as Vikramajita as well as Ratna Singh, her father, at separate places: 'Many sadhus and holy men came to visit Mīrā, and because of this Vikramajita ill-treated her', and (at another place) 'she was an unswerving devotee of Krishna and showed the utmost reverence for saints and sadhus. Ratna Singh was greatly annoyed by this and tormented her.' It is unimagina-ble, however, that her own father could go to the extreme extent of poisoning her. Apparently, though Ratna Singh might have dis-approved of her conduct, her tormentor was not her father, but her brother-in-law. Nothing can be more authentic than her own observation about it. In one of her songs she says, 'If the Rāṇā is displeased with me, the most he can do is to make me leave his domain. But if I displease Krishna, where can I go? The Rāṇā sent me a cup of poison. I drank it taking it to be nectar.'[22] Obviously Vikramajita is meant. Nabhadasa's *Bhaktamālā* gives more details: 'Considering it a fault, that evil-minded man determined to kill her. But it did not come about. She drank the poison sent by him as though it was nectar. Another attempt to kill her was made by Vikramajita by sending her a wicker-basket with a deadly cobra inside it. But when she opened the lid, lo! there was a Vishnu-idol in place of the serpent.'[23] One can't discard legend and tradition in the lives of saints, particularly when historical evidence is lacking, or is of a conflicting nature. But a distinction must be made between legend and exaggeration. For example, taking the cue from the episode about the cobra, one writer has given a long list of poisonous creatures and instruments of torture, which would outdo those of a torture-chamber! that he believed Vikramajita devised for Mīrā—snakes, scorpions, hungry lions and even centipedes![24] Apart from Mīrā's own songs there are references to Vikramajita's attempts to kill her in the works of various poets such as Priyadasa, Dhruvadasa, Nabhadasa and Dayā Bāī.[25] It was only the protecting hand of her Beloved Krishna which could defeat all such evil designs.

KRISHNA UNION

Meanwhile, unmindful of all these acts of animosity, Mīrā was passing through what the Vaishnavas call the *mādhurya* stage of devotion in which love for God takes the nature of a husband-wife or lover-beloved kind of relationship. The Sufis, who had begun to raise their voice, and preached a creed of the same kind, also believed in such union. The great Sufi mystic, Jalal-ud-din Rumi said, 'A man went to the Beloved and standing by the door, knocked. "Who is there?" the Beloved asked. He said, "It is I." The voice from inside answered, "Go away, there is no room here for Me and Thee". After sometime the man came again and knocked. When asked who was there, he said "It is Thee." Then the door opened.' Mīrā was with her Lord and her Lover in the same way. She was fully aware that human birth, as Shankaracharya said in the *Vivekacūḍāmaṇi,* is obtained with great difficulty, and that one who having got it, does not seek God, is a fool who slays his own self. As she says in one of her verses 'One cannot get emancipation without devotion to Rāma. Without it, he has to come back to the earth and pass through eighty-four lakh births in the world.'[26] With this belief strong in her, Mīrā surrendered herself to Krishna body and soul. In such surrender she found God, for as Krishna says in the *Gītā*, 'He who surrenders all works to me and has unwavering faith in me, and worships me with single-minded devotion, is loved by me; and I quickly come to rescue him from this worldly sea of sorrows.'[27] Krishna was everything to her, and she fancied herself as wedded to him. She would wait nights for him on her rooftop, as a girl pining for her lover. She saw Krishna in a vision. He came to her as a bridgegroom and she fancied she was wedded to him with all the ceremonies attending marriage. Ever since that moment she considered herself to be Krishna's bride and used to weep for him night and day, till her tired eyes became red with lack of sleep. People started slandering her and the school of scandal buzzed with activity. The smear campaign was on. Men who are of small minds and securely tied with the ropes of greed and lasciviousness, are out of tune with the Infinite. They cannot understand such a union. No wonder then that the royal house of Mewāṛa was agog with rumours that Mīrā had besmirched the honour of the clan of Rāṇās. An attempt was even made to poison Vikramajita's ears with a false charge against her, and it was easily done, for as we have said there was no love lost between them. Mīrā's sister-in-law (husband's sister), Ūdābāī, tried her best to dissuade her from going to sadhus and dancing in the temples. But all her admonitions had no effect on Mīrā, who would often keep awake and in the late hours of night, speak rapturously to the image of Giradhara which she had acquired in her childhood. Ūdābāī was aware of this, and taking advantage of the sweet nothings Mīrā spoke to the image, she played a mean trick on her. She falsely accused Mīrā of admitting a man in her apartment when all was quiet, and in the dead of night making love to him in the lamp's light. When Vikramajita heard this trumped up charge he was filled with rage, and drawing his sword, went to Mīrā's room and shouted, 'Where is that lover of yours? Show me where he is. I will slay him and you too, you dissembling wretch! Don't try to deceive me, I distinctly heard you talking to someone.' Mīrā, who was ever lost in the love of Krishna, coolly pointed to the image and said, 'I was addressing my Lord Giradhara. He is my eternal Beloved. I know no man. My Lover is Krishna. Don't you see him smiling at me. Ah! he stretches his arms to embrace me. I have surrendered everything to him—my body, my heart and my soul.' Thus Mīrā raved on, quite unmindful of the naked sword in Vikramajita's hands. Evidently the Rāṇā could find no trace of a hidden lover in the room or anywhere else, and so he departed.

FAREWELL TO MEWĀRA

Mīrā's cup of misery was full. She could not ever be in tune with the stately atmosphere of the royal household in which worldliness crowded out piety and all that went on was tied up with the lust for power and the pursuit of sensual pleasures. She made a hard decision, and that was to leave Mewāra and go to her maternal home, Meṛatā. There she could live in peace, spending her days in her rapturous devotion to Krishna. Her uncle, Rao Viramdeva and her cousin Jayamala were very cordial to her and she could freely move among saints and sadhus; and indeed she was often in their company. About the period of her life there the *Research Journal* says: 'Many Vaishnavas would come there. Some of them stayed for eight days, some had arrived ten days before and others had been staying for as many as fifteen days as guests in the palace.'[28] Mīrā worshipped her Lord Giradhara without any restraint, pouring out her effusions of ecstatic love and adoration before his image.

VRINDAVANA AND DVARAKA

Meanwhile events were moving fast in Meṛatā. The long-standing enmity between the rulers of Jodhpur and Meṛatā erupted in war between the two states, and in AD 1538 Rao Maladeva, ruler of Jodhpur, extended his suzerainty to Meṛatā. This again jeopardized Mīrā's freedom to move among holy men and to dance in the temples before the idol of Krishna. So she decided to leave Meṛatā and set out for Vrindavana. In that sacred city associated with Krishna, she danced rapturously in the numerous Krishna-temples there, ankle-bells on feet, clapping her hands in tune and often punctuating her melodious songs with the clashing of cymbals. She forgot everything else. It was as though the whole world had become Krishna for her.

The renowned sage, Jiva Goswami, was in Vrindavana at this time and Mīrā was eager to meet him. But he had taken a vow not to cast his eyes on a woman. When she came to know of it she got the following message conveyed to him: 'I had thought till now that there is only one Person in Vrindavana who is a male and all the others are, as it were *gopīs* (his unswerving devotees, the cowherd-maids of Vrindavana). I have known only today that there is also a man here who thinks himself to be separate from the Lord'[29] Taking Mīrā's profound words to heart, Jiva Goswami hastened to meet her. Mention of this incident has been made by Priyadasa as well.[30] Mīrā Bāī was in constant touch with the sage thereafter. Near about AD 1542 she left Vrindavana for Dvaraka, another city associated with Krishna, and lost herself in the Lord's devotion.[31]

Mīrā's cousin, Jayamala, had succeeded in wresting back Meratā from Rao Maladeva and he wished her to return, sending many messengers to persuade her to come back. But by this time she was completely detached from the world and deeply immersed in the love of Krishna: *maiṁ giradhara rangarātī* as she said in one of her *padas* (verses).[32] Although Jayamala's messengers tried their utmost to convince her that she should come to Meratā, and even openly protested against her decision not to leave Dvaraka, she was firm in her resolve. As Nagaridasa records: 'The messengers reached Dvaraka and stayed there many days. They said to her, "You have been away for long, now please return (to Meratā). The Rāṇā has ordered thus." They said this many a time and even refused to return without her'.[33] Nonetheless Mīrā had made up her mind, and the messengers had to go back disappointed. As for Mīrā, she had realized her life's aim and had experienced unbroken bliss in Krishna-union.

MĪRĀ'S DEATH

Mīrā stayed on at Dvaraka, and according to traditional belief was absorbed in the image of Krishna in the temple there: 'Then Mīrā, minded to say farewell to Shri Raṇachore (Krishna) went alone to the temple and sang two songs in adoration. When she had finished, the Lord, Krishna, absorbed her completely in Himself. Not a trace of her mortal body remained.'[34] This is, of course, the account of her end as popularly believed. It is not collaborated by historical evidence. Indeed just as for Mīrā's birth, the date of her death, too, is shrouded in mystery, there being many inferences and views, but no positive evidence. According to Munshi Devi-prasada her death took place in AD 1546, while Bharatendu Harishchandra puts it at 1573. Dr Shrikrishnalal says that there is evidence to show that Harirama Vyasa came to meet her at Mewāra in 1565. Hence she remained alive for some period after that. However most scholars agree with the date given by Deviprasada, namely AD 1546, though even this is based on a statement of one Bhuradani and so is second-hand evidence. Some scholars of Gujarati like E.S. Desai, Dr Ramakumara Varma and Dr Shrikrishnalal share the view of Bharatendu, that Mīrā died in AD 1573. Dr Shrikrishnalal says: 'It seems unlikely that Mīrā died at an early age.' Viyogi Hari is of the view that she died near about AD 1569 and Kunwar Krishnadasa gives the date as 1573, which means that Mīrā lived till the age of 73, which is most unlikely and unsupported by other evidence. Though one view is that Mīrā died early, the consensus of opinion is that she lived till the age of forty-six and died in 1546. We may accept this view as being the most likely though it might still be just a guess.

There are many traditional beliefs about the way of her death. We have spoken about one, according to which she merged with the image of Krishna. Yet another view is that the spirit of the Lord entered her eyes and they closed forever.[35] In all probability Mīrā died a peaceful death with the image of Krishna in her heart and his name on her lips. And she was at last united with him, for as he himself says in the *Gītā*, 'He who relinquishes the body remembering me, without doubt comes to me.'[36]

REFERENCES

1. G.A. Grierson, *The Modern Vernacular Literature of Hindustan*.

2. Padmavati, *Mīrāṁ Vyaktitva aur Kṛtitva*, pp. 139 et seq.

3. *Research Journal*, Kurukshetra Vishvavidyalaya, 1970, p. 89.

4. Parashuram Chaturvedi, *Mīrābāī kī Padāvalī*, p. 18.

5. Krishnadeva Sharma, *Mīrābāī-Padāvalī*, p. 8.

6. *Research Journal*, Kurukshetra Vishvavidyalaya, p. 91.

7. Sharma, *Mīrābāī-Padāvalī*, op. cit., pp. 9-10.

8. *Pūcheṁ pitā-mātā, paṭa ābharana lījiye jū |* and *roya milī mahatārī, kahī lījiye laṛāyekai |*

9. 'Duda's daughter was the celebrated Mīrā Bāī' and 'Ratna Singh was Mīrā's father'.

10. *Mīrā ke Jīvana-vṛtta kā Sthānīya Sākṣya—Mīrāṁ-smṛti*.

11. Purohit H. Sharma, *Brajnidhi Granthāvalī*.

12. According to Krishnadeva Sharma (*Mīrā-Padāvalī*) Mīrā's mother died when Mīrā was a child of two years.

13. This is evident from *Mīrābāī kī Shabdāvalī*.

14. J.N. Farquhar, *An Outline of the Religious Literature of India*, pp. 205-6.

15. *The Cultural Heritage of India*, vol. 2, p. 252.

16. J.C. Oman, *The Mystical Asiatics and Saints of India*, p. 100.

17. G.A. Grierson, *The Modern Vernacular Literature of Hindustan*.

18. See, for example, *The Songs of Mīrā*, verse 8—*maiṁ giradhara ranga rātī*.

19. Ibid., verse 22—*maiṁ giradhara āgāṁ nācuṁ rī* |
20. *Rāṇo bhejyā viṣro pyālā caranāmṛta pī jānā* | Dr Padmavati expresses the view that it was Mīrā's husband who was cruel to her not Vikramajita. But this does not seem likely at all (*Mīrāṁ Vyaktitva aur Kṛtitva*), p. 153.
21. Padmavati, op. cit., p. 151.
22. *The Songs of Mīrā*, verse 43.
23. *Kālā nāga piṭārī bhejyā, salagarāma pichānā* | *mīrā to aba prema divānī, sāṁvaliyā vara pānā* | ('He sent me a black cobra which I took to be a *sāligarāma*. I am drunk with the love of my Dark Lord who is my Beloved.') A *sālagrāma* is a Krishna-idol shaped as a smooth oval stone (not cylindrical, as the Shiva-linga).
24. Ananda Swarupa, *Mīrāṁ Sudhā-sindhu-swāmī*, pp. 49-58.
25. *Bandhuni viṣa tākoṁ diyo, kari vicāra citta jāno* | *so viṣa phira amṛta bhayau taba lāge pachitānī* | (Dhruvadasa)
   Garala paṭhāyau sau tau sīsa lai caṛhāyo | *saṅga tyāga viṣa bhārī, tāko jhāra na samāri hai* | (Priyadasa)
   Duṣṭani doṣa vicāri, mṛtyu ko udidama kiyo | *bara na baṁko bhayo, garala amṛta jyoṁ pīyo* | (Nabhadasa)
   Viṣa kā pyālā ghola ke, rāṇā bhejyo chāna | *mīrā āṁ cayo rāma kahi, ho gayo sudhā samāna* | (Dayā Bāī)
26. *Songs of Mīrā*, verse 52, *rāmā nāmā bina mukati na pāvai, phira caurāsī jāvai* |
27. *Bhagavadgītā*, 12.6-7.
28. *Research Journal*, Kurukshetra Vishvavidyalaya, p. 94.
29. Venketeshvara, *Chaurāsī Vaishnava kī Vārtā*, p. 342.
30. Parashurama Chaturvedi, op. cit., p. 233.
31. Dvaraka means 'The city of gates'. It was Krishna's capital in Gujarat, and was thought to have been submerged by the ocean seven days after his death. It is one of the seven sacred cities.
32. *Songs of Mīrā*, verse 8.
33. *Purohita dvārakā pahuṁce, tahāṁ kaī dina raheṁ to pīche mīrāṁbāī ke saṅga prauhitādik ne rāṇā ke loka he tīna kahyau aba bahuta dina bhaye haiṁ deśa ko calī, rāṇā kī ājñā hai* | *jaise dvau tīna to kahyau* | *phira mīrāṁbāī pari dharanā kiyo* |
34. Krishnadeva Sharma, op. cit., pp. 16-17—'*taba hī ṭhākura (śrī raṇachoṛe) āpa meṁ unako yāhī sarīra taiṁ līne, dehahū na rahīṁ* |'
35. Bhagawanadasa Tiwari, *Mīrā kā Kāvya*, p. 41—*kṛṣṇa unakī āṁkhoṁ meṁ ākara samā gaye, palakeṁ khulī kī khulī raha gaīṁ aura mīrā kṛṣṇamaya ho gaī* | This conclusion is based on a verse of hers which says that she will enshrine Krishna's image in her eyes and will not lower them for fear it may vanish (*Songs of Mīrā*, verse 62—*naina na banaja basāūṁ rī*). But this emphasizes only her desire for Krishna-union and cannot be construed as relating to her death.
36. *Bhagavadgītā*, 8.5.

3

Some Knotty Points

Before we close this brief account of Mīrā's life, it would be appropriate to clear some misconceptions about certain incidents which are erroneously said by some writers to have taken place involving her.

Akbar and Tansen

One of these is about Akbar and Tansen (the renowned singer) meeting her. The commentaries of Priyadasa and Raghavadasa on the *Bhaktamālā* refer to such a meeting.[1] But it could not possibly have taken place, for Akbar was born on 23 November 1542 and Mīrā, as we have concluded, died in 1546, when Akbar was four years old. Such a meeting, therefore could not have taken place and is a myth.

Mīrā and Tulsidasa

Another controversy relates to a letter which, according to Baba Benimadhavadasa, Mīrā wrote to Tulsidasa, the author of the *Rāmacaritmānasa,* seeking his advice and words of comfort, when the oppression on her by her brother-in law became unbearable. She is said to have sent a message in verse to Tulsidasa telling him about the ill-treatment: 'The people of my own household have greatly multiplied my troubles.'[2] It is said that Tulsidasa wrote back saying that she should seek comfort in Rāma, giving the instance of Prahlada, Vibhishana, Bharata and Bali, all of whom were oppressed in one way or the other, yet found peace. The verses ascribed to Tulsi are doubtless his, but they can hardly be associated with Mīrā as Benimadhava says.[3] Tulsidasa was doubtless a poet of renown (*mahākavi*) and apparently the writer has associated him with Mīrā to enhance her fame. The letter and Tulsi's reply are just fanciful. It is said that this exchange of letters took place in 1559, which would be thirteen years after Mīra's death. So the entire episode is an anachronism and purely imaginative.

MĪRĀ'S GURU

Yet another matter which has been commented on by scholars is about Mīra's guru. Various names have been suggested, such as Raidasa,[4] Tulsidasa, Vitthalanatha, Jiva Goswami and so forth. Occasional references are found in Mīra's songs to Raidasa and Vitthala. Raidasa's period of life is reckoned to be 1394 to 1418. Thus he lived much before Mīra. The reference to him is out of respect, for she had great reverence for all those sages who were near God. The same is the case with Vitthala, which is, in fact a name for Lord Vishnu. In truth her guru was not a human being at all. Saints like Chaitanya, Ramadasa, Ramakrishna and so forth have no need for any human intervention between them and God. To them God speaks himself, because when his devotee has true love for him, he seeks them out, speaks to them, ministers to them and discloses himself to them. Mīra was one of such devotees. Her whole existence was bound with Krishna. To her he was not merely a name. She actually saw him and lived with him. As Kabir says, 'Lifting the curtain I have seen.'

REFERENCES

1. *Rūpa kī nikāī bhūpa akbar bhāī hiye| liye saṅga tānasena dekhibo ko āyo hai| nirakhi nihāla bhayo, chabi giridhārīlāl| pada sukha jāla eka taba hī caṛhayo hai||* (Priyadasa) *Bhūpa akbar rūpa sunyau ati tanahisena līye cali āyau| deṣi kusyala bhayo lālahi eka sabado banāi sunāyau ||* —(Raghavadas)
2. *Ghara ke svajana hamāre jete, sabana upādhi baṛhāī |*
3. The concerned verse is: *taba āyo mewāṛa te, vipranāma sukhapāla| mīrābāī patrikā lāyo prema prabāla|| paṛhi pāto uttara likhe, gati kavitta banāya| saba taji hari bhajibo kahi diya vipra paṭhāya ||*
4. *Mīrāṁ ne govinda milyā jī, guru milyā raidāsa | mahāroṁ guru raidāsa jī, dīnhiṁ jñāna kī guṭakī ||* and *kāśī nagara yā coka yā mane guru milyā raidāsa |*

4

What Mīrā Wrote About

More than four hundred years ago, God sent on earth a puppet of his love. She came immersed in the love of God, held fast in his embrace and merged with his form, uniting her heart with the jingle of ankle-bell, pouring out her soul in the notes of his flute, held spellbound by his yellow garment of silk and his soft smiles, laying open her heart to him as though a carpet for his feet to tread on;—thus that artless *yoginī*, ankle-bells on her feet and cymbals in her hands, danced away and sang on, intoxicated with the ecstasy of love.*—B.N. Mishra 'Madhava'

THE NATURE AND LANGUAGE OF MĪRĀ'S POETRY

In his letter to John Taylor of 27 February 1818 John Keats wrote, 'If poetry comes not as naturally as leaves to a tree, it had better not come at all', and in the Preface to his *Lyrical Ballads* William Wordsworth remarked, 'Poetry is the spontaneous overflow of powerful feelings'. Further, poetry, and for that matter prose too, appeals most when it is written in homespun language, which is the one which is commonly spoken and understood. That is the reason why, despite all its scholarship, the Valmiki's *Rāmāyaṇa* is not so popular as Tulsi's. Mīrā's poetry, which indeed is nearer to music than to verse, fulfils all these requirements. It comes from the heart, as all great poetry should. Her *padas* are predominantly an expression of her oneness with Krishna and generally end with the words 'Mīrā's Lord is none other than Giradhara (Krishna)'. It is through love that she communes with God. While other poets only spoke of the truth, she *knew,* and her poetry was 'music sent up to God by the lover and the bard.'[1] But occasionally she also wrote *padas* in a philosophical vein, ruminating on the evanescence of existence and

---

*Author's translation.

bemoaning the worldliness of people. 'Everything that exists, perishes' she says, 'the sun, the moon, earth and sky—only the One Imperishable remains forever'[2] (recalling Shelley's line, The One remains, the many change and pass). 'No one can escape destiny' she says, giving the examples of Harishchandra, Draupadi and Bali to prove her point.[3] Commenting on the mysteriousness of the ways of God, she says, 'He causes fools to be rulers and learned men to go about begging for food.'[4] She likens worldly existence to a dream or a dried ocean (much in the spirit of the Advaitist, Shankara), 'a cauldron of ills' or 'a game of dice which ends when the night comes.'[5] Speaking of men who are too much with the world, she says, 'Men will walk miles and miles, but they are loath to go a short distance to pray in a temple. They will hasten to watch a nautch, but will never chant God's name.'[6] She ridicules those who mechanically count the rosary, their minds wandering elsewhere. Do they think, she asks them, that the All-knowing God will heed such empty prayer?[7] She asks people to be content with what they have—their homes, their fields and so forth—and not to be envious of the riches of others.[8] Thus Mīrā's poetry depicts the versatility of her genius. Although most of her *padas* are about Krishna-union, a good few reach the height of spirituality.

Mīrā also wrote about the loveliness and grandeur of nature. Some of her *padas* are almost exclusively descriptions of such natural beauty. In one of them she gives a description of the changing seasons, month after month.[9] She gives charming descriptions of the rains: 'Clouds rush from every side and streaks of lightning flash across the sky. The cool easterly breeze blows, bringing showers.'[10] 'The wind loses its gentleness and starts roaring fiercely, and the sky is darkened with clouds.'[11] 'The rain pours and pours, flooding the land all round with water. The withered plants revive and are clad in green.'[12] 'The naked lightning rushes shamelessly to embrace the bare earth.'[13] 'The tiny drops of rain fall drip, drip, drip.'[14] Mīrā's descriptions of nature are superb, and often have a Wordsworthian touch.

As for Mīrā's dates of birth and death, scholars are also divided regarding the language in which she wrote. She conformed to no particular school of poetry and, as we have said, had no guru. Her songs were sung in various assemblies of sadhus in many parts of the country, giving the dialect a twist to conform to the one spoken there. Even the number of verses attributed to her varies beyond all measure. The collection of Dakor and Kashi has 103 and the *Mīrā-sudhā-sindhu* has 1,312. Various other anthologies with refrains of *Mīrā ke prabhu giradhara nāgara* and *Mīrā ke prabhu hari avināsī*, have as many as 5,197 verses, of which 3,797 are in Devanagari and 817 in Gujarati.

Munshi Deviprasada has mentioned four works which he attributes to Mīrā—a commentary on the *Gīta-govinda*, *Narasījī Maharā*, a collection of verses of which some are said to be hers, and *Rāgasarotha-pada-saṁgraha*. Of these the first, the commentary on *Gīta-govinda*, was written by Rāṇā Kumbha, not Mīrā. The others are either not extant, or do not appear to be hers, while the anthology comprises the verses of many other poets as well. In his *Hindī Sāhitya kā Itihāsa*, Acharya Ramachandra Shukla has ascribed a book titled *Rāga-govinda* to Mīrā.[15] But there is no *rāga* (tune) known as Govinda in Indian music. It could be that he means thereby some anthology of Mīrā's *padas*. Relying on the views of G.H. Ojha and K.N. Jhaveri, Acharya Parashurama Chaturvedi has attributed two works to Mīrā, namely *Mīrāṁbāī kā Malāra* and *Garvāgītā* (or *Mīrāṁ nī Garbī*, according to Brijratnadasa), but none of these works are extant.

There are some handwritten scripts in various libraries and societies which have a few *padas* bearing Mīrā's name. These are at Jodhpur in the collection of the ruler of that place (the *Pustaka Prakāśa*); the Puratattva Mandir, Jodhpur; Ramadvara; Dholi Bavali, Udaipur; the Phaṁbāsa Gujarat Sabhā, Bombay; the Gujarat Vernacular Society, Ahmedabad, and at various other places. However these do not have any of Mīrā's *padas* even though some bear her name. They appear to be, as one writer says, the compositions of other saints and poets.[16]

Dr I.J. Sorabji Taraporewala says about Mīrā's poetry:

Mīrā's songs have been current in three vernaculars—Hindi, Marwari and Gujarati. And during the centuries that have elapsed since her time, a great deal of mixing of dialects in her songs has come about. It is probable, however, that she herself a Rajputani, used the mixture of these three dialects in her later years. But her very popularity in these three vernaculars has made it extremely difficult to determine what is her own genuine work and what is later forgery.[17]

Dr Bhagawandasa Tiwari's view is that Mīrā wrote her *padas* in

Marwari only.

> Those which are said to be hers and are in Hindi or Gujarati are either fabricated or wrongly attributed to her...those which bear her name and are in Rajasthani, are also not hers.[18]

According to one view Mīrā's songs were not written or compiled at all. The sadhus and holy men in whose company she moved, jotted them down and that's how they have come to us. Dr Padmavati says that in the documents available in the Loka Sahitya Vidyalaya, Girinara, it is mentioned that Mīrā's verses have been handed down primarily through Bhils and other such tribals. 'However in the two *padas* finding place in the documents of the Vidyalaya which are ascribed to her (one about Rāṇā Kumbha and the other regarding Raidasa) none appears to be hers, for the language used in them is quite different from Mīrā's.'[19] The Girinara record also relates an incident which is not only amusing but also trumped up. According to this Mīrā came to Raidasa to persuade him to go to Chittor with her, but he was unwilling to go, for he feared he would be unwelcome because of his low-caste. At that time he was cleaning a buffalo's skin and by chance a drop of the beast's blood fell on her dress. She was repelled and horrified and tried to clean it away. But the stain would not go. Raidasa asked her to suck it away and when she did so it disappeared and she had knowledge of *Brahman*. As we have said, Raidasa lived much earlier than Mīrā and the question of their meeting does not arise. So this fantastic and ludicrous story can be dismissed as purely imaginative, and it also confirms Dr Padmavati's premise that the Girinara records are not authentic. The idea that Mīrā's *padas* were handed down by Bhils and tribals, too, is fanciful and ought to be dismissed as myth.

The truth seems to be that Mīrā composed her songs in at least three dialects, namely Rajasthani, Gujarati and Brajabhasha (the language of the Braja country, i.e., Vrindavana and Mathura). She belonged to Mewāra and so it is quite natural that she wrote most of her poetry in the Marwari dialect of Rajasthan. She lived in Vrindavana and in her latter years in Dvaraka, so she must have composed some of her verses in the language spoken in these places too—Braja and Gujarati.

REFERENCES

1. Robert Browning, *Abt Vogler*.
2. *Songs of Mīrā, pada* 45.
3. Ibid., *pada* 41.
4. Ibid., *pada* 34.
5. Ibid., *padas* 2, 52 and 57.
6. Ibid., *pada* 72.
7. Ibid., *pada* 80.
8. Ibid., *pada* 26, cf. Kabir, *rūkhā sūkhā khāi ke ṭhaṇḍā pānī pīva | dekha birāni cūparī mata lalacāvai jīva ||*
9. *Songs of Mīrā, pada* 46.
10. Ibid., *pada* 65.
11. Ibid., *pada* 66.
12. Ibid., *pada* 56.
13. Ibid., *pada* 37.
14. Ibid., *pada* 13.
15. Ramchandra Shukla, *Hindī Sāhitya kā Itihāsa*, p. 184.
16. Bhagawandasa Tiwari, *Mīrāṁ kī Bhakti aur unakī Kāvya-sādhanā kā Anuśīlan*, pp. 29-39.
17. I.J. Sorabji Taraporewala, *Selections from Classical Gujarati Literature*, vol. 1, p. 372.
18. Bhagawandasa Tiwari, *Mīrāṁ kā Kāvya*, p. 65. (English trans. author's)
19. *Mīrāṁ Vyaktitva aur Krititva*, Appendix 13, p. 502. The verses are:
    (1) *uttarākhaṇḍa thī eka caraṇa āyo | māṁge kumbhā kerī rāṇī | bhalo re bhalo mewāṛa gaṛh no rāṇo kumbho | kumbha sarīkhā harijana amana he te malo | kumbha sarīkho rājiyo | ene sola sau rāṇī | uttarākhaṇḍa thī eka caraṇa ayo | (2) mīrān bāī rāṭhorā nī kunvarī | rohīdāsā jāta na camāra | mīrān bāī gher jāo ne | ghere baise rādhesyāma | cittauṛ ke re cauka mā mīrān bāī | bāto evī thāya | cittoṛa jānasī to māṛusī | thāmṛ cope karasī bāta ||*

5

Mīrā's Poetical Art

Mīrā's poetry may be termed lyrical verse, which, Earnest Rhys says, 'is a form of musical utterance in words governed by overmastering emotion and set free by a powerfully concordant rhythm.'[1] In fact the lyric was sung to the accompaniment of the lyre. In some recensions Mīrā's songs are classified according to specific tunes *(rāgas)*. This does testify to their musical quality, but it is very doubtful if she herself classified them under such heads. Quite possibly the editors of later anthologies arranged them that way. That they could do so shows, however, that they were more songs *(gīta)* than mere poetry *(kavitā)*. This should not be taken to mean that what she wrote was not poetry. It was that too, and it was poetry of the highest order. Hindi poets use *alaṁkāras* in polishing up their verse. It's much like adorning a woman in fine clothes and ornaments, and may be termed 'embellishment'. It is often understood as figures of speech. It is that too, but much more. A Hindi dictionary calls it 'those devices which establish such a relation between word and meaning as add to the charm of poetry.'[2] Mīrā's songs make use of *alaṁkāras* which broadly fall under three heads—*śabda alaṁkāra* (the adornment of words); *artha alaṁkāra* (heightening the effect of poetry by subtleness of meaning, as Keats advised Shelley to do: 'be more of an artist, and load every rift of your subject with ore');[3] and third, *ubhaya alaṁkāra* (from *ubhaya,* meaning 'both' or 'two'), i.e., the perfect fusion of both word and meaning. We find a number of figures of speech in Mīrā's songs, like alliteration: *samarath saraṇa tumhārī saiyaṁ, saraba sudhāraṇa kāja* |; repetition of words to emphasize what is meant: *rāma nāma rasa pījai manuāṁ, rāma nāma rasa pījai* | (there is alliteration as well as repetition in this), and in her oftquoted line, *jogī mata jā, mata jā, mata jā, pāṁi parūṁ maiṁ terī cerī hoṁ* |; comparisons using both metaphor and simile, for example: *aṁsuvaṁ jala sīṁca sīṁca prema beli boī* |[4] and *jyoṁ cātaka ghana kom raṭai, machari jyom pānī ho | mīrā vyākula virahiṇī sudha-budha bisarānī ho ||;*[5] comparisons of the abstract with the concrete, as for example, *āli samvaro kī dṛṣṭa mānum prema kī kaṭārī hai |*[6] We have examples of *artha alamkāras* also in her songs, as for instance the one in which she says that the agony of her longing for Krishna can be known only by one who has undergone such agony, as only one wounded can know how a wound pains and only a jeweller can recognize a genuine gem.[7] The verse expresses Mīrā's agony very graphically. Only those who have undergone grief can understand the grief of others. This is also what Lord Krishna says to Arjuna in the *Gītā,* 'He who suffers the sorrows of every creature in his own heart, I consider to be the best of yogis.'[8] And Socrates says, 'We need the ministrations of physicians in sickness and of friends in sorrow.'[9] Thus Mīrā conveys in this verse the high and noble expression of thought which has the sacredness of the scriptures and the reach of great thinkers, and is a perfect example of *śabda alamkāra.* Then there is the use of *ubhaya alamkāra,* the complete fusion of word and meaning. It is as Tulsidasa says in the *Rāma-caritmānasa: girā aratha jala bīci sama, kahiata bhinna na bhinna* ('That which is like the word and its meaning, or like water and its wave; seemingly separate but in truth one').[10] This perfect fusion between word and meaning is one of the qualities which elevates Mīrā's *padas* to the height of rhapsody. An example is the *pada* in which she says: 'I can't sleep without my Beloved. The agony of parting afflicts me and the ardour is like a consuming fire. I delight in my Lover alone, and without him I toss about restlessly in bed all night.'[11]

Mīrā uses variations of words to enhance the melody of her songs. For example, *muraliyā* in place of *muralī* (the flute), *govindā* in place of *govinda* (a name of Krishna), *papaiyā* instead of *papihā* (the sparrow-hawk), *ghumgharyā* for *ghumghrū* (a girdle of bells worn round the ankles). Similarly she coins new words like *hibaro* for *hṛdaya* (the heart), *neharā* for *sneha* (love), *nirata* for *nṛtya* (dance), and *nidar* for *nidrā* (sleep). Other such instances can be found throughout her verses. She often adds a syllable or word, like *ṇ* or *ain* in order to fit in the line with the melody.

Most critics are of the view that Mīrā did not deliberately choose her words to create an effect, rather her poetry was the spontaneous outpouring of her heart, and achieved perfection because of her artless and deep emotions. Nonetheless it can't be said that the words just tumbled out of themselves. That is too good to be true. Musicians and singers often frequented royal households. Till Mīrā's time they had not reached Moghul durbars, as they did in the age of Akbar, and they were mostly patronized by Hindu princes who were still in the twilight of their glory. So Mīrā must have been taught music in her early years and perhaps dancing too. Besides she moved about in the company of sadhus, singing and dancing before the images in temples. Thus the musical element came automatically to her. But she must have suited her words to the melody too, for without having done so her songs could not have conformed so closely to the various *ragas* and been so perfect as to be sung as *bhajans* (religious songs). It was perhaps a little of both, for spontaneity without art would be a mere flood of words, and art without spontaneity would not tug the heartstrings.

REFERENCES

1. *Lyric Poetry*, Foreword.
2. Shri Navalji, *Viśāla Śabda Sāgara*.
3. John Keats, *Letters*, 227, To Shelley, August, 1820.
4. 'I have watered the creeper of love with my tears.'
5. 'As the *cātaka* bird longs for clouds, (i.e., the first raindrops) and a fish deprived of water, for water; so too Mīrā longs for Krishna and has forgotten all else.'
6. 'Friend, Krishna's glance stabs me as though it were a dagger.'
7. *Songs of Mīrā*, *pada* 10.
8. *Bhagavadgītā*, 6.32.
9. Socrates, *Stobaeus, Florilegium*, CXIII.16.
10. Bāla Kāṇḍa, 18.
11. *Songs of Mīrā*, *pada* 11. In many of her songs Mīrā speaks of her lovesickness for Krishna, and says that she wanders about from door to door, seeking a physician to cure it. See for example, *pada* 10.

6

The Nature of Mīrā's Love

Sensual love and spiritual love are worlds apart. One pampers to the body, the other is balm for the soul. Krishna says, 'As rivers enter the sea and lose themselves in it, while the sea is ever the same, so too that man achieves peace in whom all desires are extinguished, not he who clings to his desires.'[1] The person who has reached the topmost height of spirituality, sees God everywhere. To him love becomes, in Shelley's words, a kind of worship.[2] He attains to a state of fine frenzy: 'The rustling of the wind is taken as indicating the Lord's approach, the dark blue sky, the sea and the landscape become symbolic of the colour of the Divine figure. Every sound seems to convey to him a message from the Lord, every form a sense of the Divine presence, and every touch the warmth of the Divine contact.'[3] Mīrā's love for Krishna was of this all-encompassing kind. Her Krishna was enshrined in her heart and her soul. She saw him as Shri Ramakrishna saw Mother Kali. He said to his disciple, Swami Vivekananda, 'God can be seen and talked to. One can talk to him just as I am talking to you. But who cares to do so? People shed torrents of tears for their wife and children, but who does so for the sake of God? If one weeps sincerely for him, he will surely manifest himself.' Mīrā wept for Krishna. She would spend sleepless nights tossing about in bed for a sight of him. Her heart ached for him and his image was ever in it. 'How can I stay in my home without seeing Krishna?' She wrote.[4] Life without him was not possible, as she said in one of her verses, 'Friend, I can't live without Krishna.'[5] That indeed is the mark of true love, for:

'Love is not love
When it is mingled with regards that stand
Aloof from the entire point.'[6]

Mīrā had indeed 'sold' herself Krishna, as she put it in many of her verses, meaning thereby that she had surrendered herself completely to him. Though she knew that tongues would be wagging and people would malign her—*loga kahaiṁ bigaṛī*—her surrender was so complete that she never cared for what they said. The union of the lover and the beloved is the highest expression of love.

> Love in which there's laughter and sobbing,
> Moaning, throbbing and clasping in tight embrace,
> That alone is liberation for me,
> I care for no other.[7]

The Hindu attitude to love is often misunderstood in the West: 'The worship of Shiva with its undisguised emphasis upon the generative organs of both sexes, the *liṅga* and the *yoni*, does not strike the Hindu, however young and innocent, as obscene: "obscenity" might rather be attributed to the tendency found almost universally in the Occident, namely to associate sexual operations with other purely automatic activities.'[8] Many in Mīrā's own times and even afterwards, have looked on the expression of her love for Krishna—a kind of wife-husband relationship—as corrupt, when really the corruption is in their own minds. It is the heart's purity which gives one courage, as Sir Galahad, one of the Knights of the Round Table, said.[9] So was it with Mīrā. It was her purity which gave her strength and the courage to boldly face villainy and withstand the cruel treatment of her brother-in-law and others, after her husband's death.

Maharshi Śāṇḍilya calls devotion 'ardent love of God'. Mīrā's love for Krishna was much of that kind. It permeated each pore of her body and, as she says in one of her verses, it possessed her as intimately as a dye permeates a garment—*maiṁ giradhara ranga rātī|*[10] The *Bhāgavata* enumerates nine kinds of devotion, namely, listening to the praises of the Lord; *kīrtana* or community singing, in the style of Chaitanya; remembering God's name; adoration by prostrating oneself before him; ritual worship; complete dependence on him; serving him as a slave would serve his master; looking on him as a companion or friend; and complete self-surrender.[11] The *navadhā-bhakti* (nine forms of devotion) was also disclosed by Rama to Shabari: (1) Serving the saints; (2) Love for hearing the deeds of the Lord; (3) Sitting humbly at the feet of the guru; (4) Singing the Lord's praises with a simple heart; (5) Complete faith in God and in his name; (6) Going beyond the senses, having a noble nature, renunciation and the company of saints; (7) Seeing the whole world pervaded by the Divine, and holding saints in greater esteem than God himself; (8) Being content with what one has and not finding fault with others; and (9) Simplicity, behaving with everyone without dissimulation, complete dependence on God and being the same in joy and sorrow.'[12]

We find most of these elements of devotion in Mīrā. She would move in the company of saints and listen with reverence to religious discourses: 'Lord Hari' she says, 'I have heard that you come to the rescue of the poor and the powerless and take them across the fearful ocean of birth and death.'[13] While with holy men she would also sing and dance in the temples. 'There is no joy' she says, 'for one who does not sing the praises of God.'[14] 'It is only by this that I have been able to escape this serpent-shaped existence.'[15] All religions say that God is merciful to sinners. Krishna says in the *Gītā*, 'Even though one may be greatly evil, he should be considered virtuous if he has rightly resolved.'[16] The *Holy Bible* promises forgiveness for the wrongs one does, provided he turns to God: 'In him we have redemption through his blood, the forgiveness of our trespasses, according to the riches of his grace which he lavished upon us.'[17] The *Holy Quran* says likewise, 'Say: O My servants! who have acted extravagantly against their own souls, do not despair of the mercy of God; for God forgives the sins altogether; for He is the Forgiving, the Merciful.'[18] The *Ādi Granth* says: 'Even if a man is prey to passion, anger, attachment and greed and guilty of the four cardinal sins, yes even murder; even though he has not listened to the scriptures, to devotional music or sacred verse; if he contemplates the Supreme Being even for a moment (with faith) he shall be saved.'[19] In the same way Mīrā, addressing Krishna in one of her verses, says that he comes to the relief of those who love him and pray to him even though they be hard-hearted and lacking sympathy. She gives the example of sinners who called upon his name on which he rushed to their aid, among them even a common prostitute.[20] 'Friend, I remember Krishna alone' she says. 'I meditate on him, and wherever his steps fall, there will I dance.'[21] She worshipped his feet with her mind, heart and soul: 'O mind, surrender yourself to Krishna's feet, those feet tender as a lotus, which give calm and remove the burning sorrows of existence.'[22] 'Friend,' she says, 'my love is for the feet of Krishna. Without his presence I find no delight in this world, which then seems illusory like a dream. Dear Beloved mine (Krishna), I recoil from all worldly ties and seek my refuge in your holy feet.' She would worship Krishna's image in the temples of Vrindavana, and at other places where she lived. In Hindu marriages a square is made in the courtyard, formed of precious pearls, sweets, or such things as the family can afford. This is the auspicious square *(chauk)* in which the bride and the bridegroom sit. Mīrā worshipped Krishna thus: 'Dear Beloved, our love is from a previous existence, how can it ever cease to possess me? I am enraptured with your lovely form. O my neighbours and friends, Krishna is in my house. Come here and sing welcome songs for him. I have made the auspicious square for him with my tears and I have surrendered to him both my body and my mind. Beloved, I have taken refuge at your feet as your slave. I have taken the vow of remaining a maid, for I have none save you.' She makes her Giradhara food-offerings *(prasāda)* as is customary with idol-worshippers: 'O Krishna, I have brought many kinds of dishes for you. Accept my offering. I know you are the world's Preserver and have no need for anything. Yet I beseech you to eat what I have brought for you, and oblige me.' In one of her verses Mīrā dwells upon the evanescence of human existence. As a leaf once broken and fallen from the branch cannot again come back, so is life when death ends it. Addressing Krishna she says, 'You alone can release me from this existence, the end of which is certain. I am your slave. Lord, you alone can take me across this uncrossable ocean of births and deaths.'[23] In many of her verses she depicts her complete surrender to Krishna. She speaks of being his 'servant and slave, life after life.'[24] It was her desire that she should minister to him as a servant lifelong: 'O my Beloved Krishna, keep me as a servant. I will plant your garden and look after it. I will thus be able to see you every day. I will wander about the streets of Vrindavana singing your deeds. Your sight will be my wages, and the chanting of your name my earning. Devotion alone will be my property. O Beloved, my eyes are eager to see your form, with your crown of peacock feathers, clothed in your yellow silk garment and a garland of five colours round your neck—thus my Beloved goes grazing cows in Vrindavana. To please you I will grow many green arbours. I will wear a yellow sari and come to you. Beloved, I am restless for you, so meet me at midnight on the bank of Yamuna river.'

Mīrā's love for Krishna was many-faceted. She looked on him as the Lord and Creator, the Saviour, Preserver and the Supreme Being who absolved his devotees of all sins and freed them from the rounds of rebirths. More than this, however, she surrendered herself wholly to him, body, mind, heart and soul, addressing him as Dear, Darling, Lover, Beloved, Lord, Life-companion and so forth (*pīya, piyā, prītama, swāmī, sājana, janama janama ke sāthī*). She was, in the words of the *Bible*, 'as a bride adorned for her husband.'[25] She says in one of her verses: 'O Beloved, you are my life's companion through many existences and so I remember you night and day. I cannot find peace without seeing you. I go up on the roof and keep watching for your coming. My eyes have become red due to lack of sleep and because of continually weeping for you.'[26] She eagerly glances down the road expecting him each minute, weeping incessantly when she is separated from him and greeting him with tears of joy when he comes. She wishes to go with him as a girl would go to her lover or a wife to her husband's home: 'I will go to Krishna's house for he is my true lover, and when I see his charming form I can't restrain myself any longer. As soon as it is nightfall I will go to him, and come back at dawn. I will sport with him and entice him in many ways. I will wear whatever garments he gives me and eat whatever he wants me to eat. I can't stay a moment without him for our love is very deep. I will sit where he ask me to sit, and if wants to sell me to someone I will place myself in his hands.' That is the farthest surrender can go. It is this aspect of Mīrā's poetry which is predominant. She never thought herself as separate from Krishna. Though her symbolism is in places erotic, there is nothing in it of the obscene. Mīrā's love had the touch of the Divine. She had become merged in Krishna and was one with him. It was the pure kind of love the *gopīs* of Vrindavana had for him—selfless all-absorbing, immaculate and endless; love which knew no satiety. It was of the nature of which Donne wrote:

> 'Take me to you, imprison me, for I
> Except you enthrall me, never shall be free,
> Nor ever chaste except you ravish me.'[27]

REFERENCES

1. *Bhagavadgītā*, 2.70.
2. P.B. Shelley, *One Word is too Often Profaned*.
3. D.C. Sen, *Chaitanya and his Age* (slightly amended).
4. *Mīrā to giradhara bina dekhe kaise rahe ghara basike |*
5. *Helī mhāsūṁ hari bina rahyau na jāya |*
6. Shakespeare, *King Lear*, act 1, scene 1, lines 239-41.

7. *camaka tamaka hāṁsī sasaka, masaka jhapaṭa lapaṭāni |*
ye jiṁhi rati so rati mukuti, aura mukuti ati hāni || —Bihārī, *The Satasai*

8. E.W.F. Tomlin, *Great Philosophies of the East*, p. 229.

9. Lord Alfred Tennyson, *Sir Galahad,*
'My strength is as the strength of ten/Because my heart is pure.'

10. *Songs of Mīrā, pada* 8.

11. *Śrvaṇam kīrtanam viṣṇoḥ smaraṇam pāda sevanam | arcanam vandanam dāsyam*
sakhyamātmanivedanam || —(*Śrīmadbhāgavata*, 7.5.23)

12. *Rāmacaritmānasa*, Araṇya Kāṇḍa, 34.4 and 35.1-2.

13. *Mhā suṇyā hari adhama udhāraṇa | adhama udhāraṇa bhava-bhaya-tāraṇa |*

14. *Bhajana binā nara phīkā |*

15. *Gāyaṁ gāyaṁ hariguṇa nisidina, kāla byāla rī bāṁcī |*

16. *Bhagavadgītā*, 9.30.

17. *Ephesians*, 1.7.8.

18. *The Holy Quran*, trans., Muhammad Ali, 39.53.

19. *Ādi Granth*, Shri Rāga.

20. The prostitute, Jivanti, had tamed a parrot whom she taught to say 'Rama', and
in teaching it she had to often repeat that sacred name herself too. It so hap-
pened that when the messengers of the god of Death came to take her, both
she and the parrot were chanting 'Rama'. Lord Vishnu, whose incarnation Rama
is believed to be, came and took her to heaven.

21. *Sāṁvaro umarana sāṁvaro sumirana, sāṁvaro dhyāna dharūṁgī| jahāṁ jahāṁ caraṇa*
dharanidhara, tahāṁ tahāṁ nirata karūṁgī |

22. *Mana theṁ parasa hari ke caraṇa| subhaga sītala kaṁvala komala jagata jvālā haraṇa |*

23. *Lāl giradhara taraṇa tāraṇa, vega karasyo pāra | dāsī mīrā lāl giradhara, jīvanā dina*
cyāra |

24. *Mīrā hari ke hātha bikānī, janama janama kī dāsī |*

25. *The Holy Bible*, Revelations, XXI.i.

26. *Mhāṁro janama maraṇa rī sāthī, thāne nahīṁ bisarūṁ dina rātī | tuma dekhyā bina*
kala na paṛata hai, jānati merī chātī | ūṁcī caṛh caṛh pantha nihārūṁ, roya roya
aṁkhiyā rātī |

27. John Donne, *Holy Sonnets*, XIV.

7

The Songs of Mīrā

Abandoning bashfulness, not caring for what people said,
Mīrā chanted Krishna's name;
The world knows her as a mine of devotion:
A band of jingle-bells round her ankles, cymbals in her hands,
She danced away, her heart overflowing with love.
With a pure heart, she moved among devotees,
Counting the world as insignificant as a blade of grass.[*]

—*Bhaktamālā*

(*lāja chāṁri mīrā giradhara bhajī, karī na kachu kulakāni |*
soī mīrā jaga vidita prakaṭa bhakti kī khāni |
nritati nūpura bāṁdhi kai nācata le karatara |
bimala hiyo bhaktani milī tṛṇu sama gaṇi saṁsāra ||)

THE ANTHOLOGIES

Various writers and commentators have given collections of Mīrā's *padas*, which differ both in the nature of the dialect as well as in the number of the verses. Krishnadeva Sharma's *Mīrāmbāī-Padāvalī* has 231 *padas*, Vishvanath Tripathi's *Mīrā kā Kāvya*, about 100, Bhavanadasa Tiwari, 103, Padmavati *(Mīrāṁ Vyaktitva aur Kṛtitva)*, 601 and Chunnilal 'Shesha' in *Mīrā Padāvalī*, 236 verses. It is difficult to say how many are actually Mīrā's and how many are accretions.

However, this collection of eighty-one of Mīrā's *padas* aims at giving the best of these recensions. The English verse rendering follows the transliterated text, and the dialect which seemed most appropriate has been adopted. While diacritical marks have generally (except in a few word) been omitted in the narrative part of the book for the convenience of the reader, they have been given throughout in the transliteration of the *padas*. For example Krishna

---

[*]Author's translation.

has been spelt in its usual form in the part of the book about Mīrā's life and works, the transliteration of the text gives the spelling with the usually accepted marks, as Kṛṣṇa.

THE PADAS

1. *mere to giradhara gopāla*
  dūsarā na koī, sakala loka joī |
  bhāī choṛyā bandhu choṛyā, choṛyā sagā soī |
  sadhu saṅga baithi baithi loka lāja khoī |
  bhagata dekhi rāji bhaī, jagata dekhi roī |
  asavana jala sīṁca-sīṁca prema beli boī |
  dadhi matha ghṛta kāṛhi liyo, ḍara diyo choī |
  rāṇā viṣa ko pyālo bhejiyo, pīya magana hoī |
  aba to bāta phaila gaī, janai saba koī |
  mīrā prabhu lagana lagī, honī ho so hoī ||

    I know only Kṛṣṇa
    no other,
    I have nothing to do with
    relations or cousins,
    or even my brother.
      People chide me
      for moving among saints
      let them:
      I grieve for those who remain
      tied to the world,
      I love those who have
      devotion.
    I have reared
    love's creeper
    with my tears.
      I have abandoned the world
      and live for love only
      as one churning curd
      to get precious ghee.
    The Rāṇā sent me poison
    I drank it cheerfully,
    now the news goes round
    bruited in every yard,
    let it; I am bound

in love to my Lord.
>   That's all that's real for me
>   let what will be, be.

2. *bhaja mana caraṇa kamuulu avināsī |*
jaitāī dīse dharani gagana bica,
tetāī saba uṭha jāsī |
kahā bhayo tīratha vrata kīnheṁ,
kahā lie karavata kāsī |
isa dehī kā garaba na karanā,
māṭī meṁ mila jāsī |
yo sansāra cahara kī bājī,
sāṁjha paḍyā uṭha jāsī |
kahā bhayo hai bhagavā paharayā,
ghara taji bhayo sanyāsī |
jogī hoya jugati nahiṁ jānī,
ulaṭi janama phira āsī |
araja karoṁ abalā kara jore,
syāma tumhārī dāsī |
mīrā ke prabhu giradhara nāgara
kaṭo jama kī phāṁsī ||

>   O Mind, seek
>   the lotus feet
>   of the Lord Almighty:
>   nothing that exists
>   in this world lasts;
>   of what use are
>   pilgrimages and fasts,
>   of what use death in Kāsī?[1]
>>   The body you prize so much
>>   is nothing, it is only dust;
>>   life is like a game of dice
>>   which ends at dusk.[2]
>   Why don the ochre robe
>   and wander as a sannyasi?
>   'tis the mind which needs control
>   or else the man comes back
>   to this world of sorrows.
>>   O Giradhara, I'm your slave,
>>   come Master, come, make haste

> the noose of worldliness chokes me,
> cut it and set me free.

3.   *mhāṁ mohana ro rūpa lubhānī |*
sundara badana kamara dala locana,
bāṁkāṁ citavana nainā samānī |
jamanā kināre kānhā dhenu carāvāṁ
bansī bajāvāṁ mīṭhī bānī |
tana mana dhana giradhara para vārāṁ
caraṇa kaṁvala mīrā bilamāṇī ||

> *What Mīrā said to her companion*
> Lovely Kṛṣṇa,
> > eyes soft as
> > lotus-petals,
> > piping away
> > while his cows graze
> > on the Yamunā bank.
> Friend, to Kṛṣṇa
> I have surrendered
> everything;
> for his touch
> my body aches,
> my thoughts take wings,
> my eyes rush out
> to embrace him.

4.   *hamāro praṇāma bāṁke bihārī jī |*
mora mukuṭa māthe tilaka birāje,
kuṇḍala alakā kārī jī |
adhara madhura para bansī bāje,
rījha rijhāvai brajanārī jī |
yā chabi dekha magana bhaī mīrā,
mohana giravara dhārī jī ||

> Kṛṣṇa, O Lover,
> my heart goes out
> to your peacock-feathered
> crown,
> *tilaka* flashing,[3]
> earrings trembling,

shining black locks
tumbling down.
    On your lips
    your flute,
    bewitching
    with its notes
    lovelorn Braja-maids.[4]
Giradhārī[5]
I am in raptures
when I see
your lovely face.

5.   *naināṁ nipaṭa baṁkaṭa chabi aṭake*
    mere nainā nipaṭa baṁkaṭa chabi aṭake |
    dekhata rūpa madanamohana ko,
    piyata piyūkha na maṭake |
    bārija bhavāṁ alaka maṁtavarī,
    naina rūpa rasa aṭake |
    teṛhī kaṭa teṛhī kara muralī,
    teṛhī pāga lara laṭake |
    mīrā prabhu ke rūpa lubhānī,
    giradhara nāgara-naṭu-ke ||

> *What Mīrā said to her companion*
> Only Kṛṣṇa can assuage
> the hunger
> of my famished eyes;
> even though they've once feasted
> on his beauty
> vying Kāma's,[6]
> nectar-like;
> they still yearn, friend,
> again
> for his sight.
>   Lotus eyes,
>   black curls
>   that enchant,
>   strings of pearls
>   dangling
>   from his turban
>   as he stands askew

his pipe aslant.[7]

6.   *jo tuma toṛau piyā, maiṁ nahiṁ toṛuṁ |*
torī prīta tori kṛṣṇa, kauna saṁga joṛuṁ |
tuma bhae taruvara, maiṁ bhaī paṁkhiāṁ |
tuma bhae saravara, maiṁ terī machiyāṁ |
tuma bhae girivara, maiṁ bhaī cārā |
tuma bhae candā, hama bhae cakorā |
tuma bhae motī prabhu, hama bhae dhāgā |
tuma bhae sonā, hama bhae suhāgā |
'bāī mīrā' ke prabhu, braja ke bāsī |
tuma mere ṭhākur, maiṁ terī dāsī ||

> Where shall I go
> with my lost love, Kṛṣṇa,
> if you forsake me?
>> As a perch for a bird
>> a pond for a fish
>> plants for a hill
>> the moon for the partridge;[8]
>> so are you, Lover, for me.
> As the string holds the pearl
> so you hold me;
> you are the gold
> I'm its dross,
> I am your slave
> you are Braja's Lord.

7.   *cālo mana jamunā tīra |*
vā jamunā kā niramala pānī,
sītala hota sarīra |
bansī bajāvata gāvata kānhā
saṅga liyo balabīra |
mora mukuṭa pītambara sohai
kuṇḍala jhalakata hīra |
mīrā ke prabhu giradhara nāgara,
caraṇa kamala pai sīra ||

> Memories revive:
>> the Yamunā water
>> clear, cool, inviting
>> which men delight in;

                on its banks
                Kṛṣṇa wanders piping
                his brother, Balarāma,
                by his side.[9]
On his head
is a crown of peacock-feathers,
he's charmingly dressed
in yellow silk,
a diamond sparkling
in his earring.
                Giradhara is my Lord,
                for his lotus-feet
                my heart's ever yearning.

8. *maiṁ giradhara rangarātī saiyāṁ maiṁ giradhara rangarātī |*
    pacaraṁga colā pahera sakhī mai
    jhiramiṭa khelana jātī |
    vā jhiramiṭa māṁ milyo sāṁvaro,
    khola milī tana gātī |
    jinake piyā paradesa basata haiṁ,
    likha likha bhejeṁ pātī |
    merā piyā mere hiya basata hai,
    na kahūṁ ātī jātī ||

        What Mīrā said to her companion
        Friend, my heart is steeped
        In Kṛṣṇa's love,
        I wore a robe of five colours[10]
        and went to play hide-and-seek,[11]
        I saw my Dark Lover there
        and gave him my body for keeps.
                Others send letters to declare
                their love: but my Lover's in my heart,
                what need have I to go anywhere?

9. *mana re parasi hari ke caraṇa |*
    subhaga sītala kaṁvala komala,
    jagata jvālā haraṇa |
    jina caraṇa prahlāda parase,
    indra padavī dharaṇa |
    jina caraṇa dhruva aṭala kīnheṁ,
    rākhī apani saraṇa |

jiṇa caraṇa brahmāṇḍa bheṁṭyau,
nakha-sikha siri dharaṇa |
jiṇa caraṇa prabhu parasi līne,
tarī gautama gharaṇa |
jiṇa caraṇa kālināga nāthyo,
gopī-līlā-karaṇa |
jiṇa caraṇa govardhana dhāryo,
indra ko garva haraṇa |
dāsī mīrā lāl giradhara,
agama tāraṇa taraṇa ||

> O Mind,
> dwell on Hari's feet[12]
>> lovely, soft, lotus-like,
>> cooling souls burning
>> with life's miseries.
>
> Feet
>
>> which gave Indra's glory to Prahlāda,[13]
>> raised Dhruva to the skies as a star[14]
>> and danced on the head of Kāliā *nāga*.[15]
>> from which the universe came
>> adorned with splendour,
>> whose touch gave life
>> to Gautama's wife
>> who had been turned to stone.[16]
>> Of amorous Kṛṣṇa
>> disporting
>> with the Braja-maids,[17]
>> lifting Goverdhana mount
>> to humble Indra.[18]
>
> Kṛṣṇa, I'm your slave,
> take my boat across
> the uncrossable sea
> and redeem me.[19]

10. *herī maiṁ to prema divānī*
    mero darada na jānai koya |
    ghāyala kī gata ghāyala jānai,
    jo koi ghāyala hoya |
    jauhari kī gata jauhari jānai,
    kyā jānai jina koya |

sūlī ūpara seja hamārī,
kisa bidha sonā hoya |
gagana maṇḍala meṁ seja piyā kī,
kisa bidha milanā hoya |
darada kī mārī dara-dara ḍolūṁ,
vaida milā nahiṁ koya |
mīrā kī prabhu pīra miṭaigī,
jaba vaida sāṁvaro hoya ||

> *What Mīrā said to her companion*
> Friend, who can know
> my love's deep anguish?
> only one wounded
> knows how it hurts,
> only a jeweller
> knows a lost gem's worth.
>> My bed is a bed of nails
>> how can I sleep?
>> and I can't reach
>> my Lover's bed made
>> in the sky.
> I wander from door to door
> maddened with grief,
> seeking a physician
> to bring me relief.
>> Only my Dark Lord
>> can cure me, friend,
>> when he doctor's my pain
>> then only 'twill end.

11. *ramaiyā bina nīṁda na āvai |*
nīṁda na āvai viraha satāvai,
prema kī āṁca ḍhulāvai |
bina piyā jota mandira aṁdhiyāro,
dīpaka dāya na āvai |
piyā bina merī seja alūnī,
jāgata raiṇa bihāvai |
piyā kaba re ghara āvai |
dādura mora papīhā bolai,
koyala sabada suṇāvai |
ghumaṭa ghaṭā ūlara hoī āī,

dāmina damaka ḍarāvai |
nainā jhara lāvai |
kahā karūṁ kita jāūṁ morī sajanī,
bedana kūna butāvai |
biraha nāgarana morī kāyā ḍasī hai,
lahara lahara jiva jāvai |
jaṛī ghasa lāvai |
ko hai sakhī sahelī sajanī,
piya kūṁ āṇa milāvai |
mīrā ke prabhu kaba re miloge,
manamohana mohi bhāvai |
kabai haṁsa kara batalāvai ||

What Mīrā said to her companions
Without my Lover
sleep eludes me
separation's fire
consumes me.
  The temple of my heart
  is dark
  for my Lover's lamp
  does not light it
  and only its light
  can delight it.
I lie all all alone
my eyes sleep-starved,
heartless Sweetheart
when will you come home?
  Dark clouds speed
  from all sides,
  lightning streaks
  across the sky;
  frogs croak
  and peacocks cry
  the *cātakas* and the cuckoos call,[20]
  making my grief more.
  tears spring in my lovelorn eyes
  and flow endlessly.
Who'll put out
parting's fire

in which I burn?
whom shall I tell, friend,
of my plight?
My grief grows
more and more
like the mounting poison
of a cobra's bite.
>Bring me some herb
>that my pain may end,
>O mates, unite me with
>Kṛṣṇa again,
>so that he may wipe away
>my tears with his smiles.

12. *jogī mata jā mata jā mata jā*
pāṁi parūṁ maiṁ terī cerī hauṁ |
prema bhagati ko pairoṁ hī nyāro,
hama ko gaila batā jā |
agara caṁdana kī citā banāūṁ,
apane hātha jalā jā |
jala bala bhaī bhasma kī ḍherī,
apane anga lagā jā |
mīrā kahai prabhu giradhara nāgara
jota se jota milā jā ||

>O Lover Yogi,
>I, your humble slave,
>clasp your lotus-feet,
>do not go away,
>stay, Lover, stay.
>>I'm lost in love's maze
>>hasten to my side
>>and show me the way
>>be my guide.
>Yogi Lover,
>I have made a pile
>of aloewood and sandalwood
>for you to ignite;
>and in its flames
>I'll immolate
>my body for your sake.

> With my ashes smear
> your limbs; so that my light
> may unite with yours
> for every and ever.[21]

13. *barasai badariyā sāvana kī,*
sāvana kī mana bhāvana kī |
sāvana meṁ umagyo mero manavā,
bhanaka sunī hari āvana kī |
umaṛa-ghumaṛa ghana meghā āyau,
damana damake jhara lāvana kī |
nānhiṁ-nānhiṁ būṁdana mehā barase
sītala pavana suhāvana kī |
mīrā ke prabhu giradhara nāgara,
ānaṁda mangala gāvana kī |

> *What Mīrā said to her companion*
> Sāvana comes, friend,[22]
> bringing joy;
> you say my Lover's coming?
> ah! how I rejoice!
>> Dark clouds are massing
>> lightning flashing
>> across the sky;
>> droplets drizzle
>> soft and light,
>> the cool breeze fills
>> hearts with delight.
> My Lord Giradhara
> is home after long,
> come friends, come,
> welcome him with songs.

14. *ālī mhāne lage vṛndāvana nīko |*
ghara-ghara tulasī ṭhākura pūjā
darasana govindajī ko |
niramala nīra bahata jamanā meṁ,
bhojana dūdha dahī ko |
ratana siṁghāsana āpa birājai |
mugaṭa dharyo tulasī ko |
kunjana-kunjana phirata rādhika,
sabada sunata muralī ko |

mīrā ke prabhu giradhara nāgara,
bhajana binā nara phīko ||

> *What Mīrā said to her companion*
> My heart is charmed
> by Vṛndāvana
> where *tulasī* plants
> grow in every home.[23]
>> You will find temples there
>> with Kṛṣṇa's image
>> on a gem-studded throne
>> his head adorned
>> with a crown of *tulasī* leaves.
> The Yamunā water flows there
> crystal-clear;
> and you'll get milk and curd
> everywhere.
>> Rādhā wanders there[24]
>> from arbour to arbour
>> charmed by the sound
>> of Kṛṣṇa's flute;
>> the seductive notes
>> filling the air
>> lingering in every lane.
> Without Giradhara
> of what use
> is this life on earth?
> Without his name
> it has no worth,
> friend, it has been lived in vain.

15. *pāyo jī maiṁ to rāmaratana dhana pāyo |*
vastu amolaka dī mhāṁre sataguru,
kirapā kari apanāyo |
janama-janama kī puṁjī pāī,
jaga meṁ sabhī khovāyo |
sata kī nāva khevaṭiyā sataguru,
bhavasāgara tara āyo |
mīrā ke prabhu giradhara nāgara,
harakha-harakha jasa gāyo ||

> I have got wealth without end,

for I have found the gem
of Rāma-devotion.[25]
'Tis my guru's gift
and for it
I have bartered worldly pleasures;
and it is now
mine forever.
No one can ever
spend it or steal it
and day by day
it increases.
Truth is the boat of my life,
but it is tempest-tossed
on life's fearful sea,
and it will be lost
if my guru does not
take hold of the rudder
and steer it safely across
Giradhara is my Lord
whose praises devotees sing,
he is ever in the hearts
of those who love him.

16. *piyā itanī binatī suno morī* |
aurana sūm rasa batiyām karata ho,
hama se rahe cita corī |
tuma bina mere aura na koī,
maim saranāgata torī |
āvana kaha gaye ajahum na āye,
divasa rahe aba thorī |
mīrā ke prabhu kaba re miloge,
araja karūm kara jorī ||

Darling Lover,
tell me pray,
why you give your heart to others
but from me you turn away?
O Beloved, I have none
save you, to whom I can go,
who shall give me shelter, say,
Lover, if you spurn me so?

You had promised you would come
yet till now you've stayed away;
the fleeting days pass one by one,
Lover, why do you delay?
    I beseech you earnestly,
    when will you come, Lord Giradhara?
    'tis your refuge that I seek,
    come, delay no longer, Love.

17. *tanika hari citavao jo meri ora |*
    hama citvata tuma citavata nāhīṁ,
    dila ke baṛe kaṭhora |
    meṛī āsā citavani tumarī ora
    na dūjā ora |
    ūbhī ṭhāṛhi araja karata hūṁ,
    araja karata bhayo bhora |
    mīrā ke prabhu hari avināsī,
    desyuṁ praṇa aṁkora ||

You don't look at me ever
though I glance at you alone,
O cruel hearted Lover
your heart is of stone!
    You are mirrored in my eyes,
    you, none other,
    I've been hungering all night
    for your glance, Lover.
I'm tired pleading, pleading,
yet you look not my way
and now night's receding
and comes the day.
    Kṛṣṇa, you are the Lord
    beginningless
    and endless;
    I will seek
    deliverance
    at your feet.

18. *māī mheṁ govinda līnī mola |*
    koī kahai chane, koī kahai chupakai,
    liyo rī bājatāṁ ḍhola |
    koī kahai sasto, koī kahai maṁhago,

līnī tarājū tola |
koī kahai kāro, koī kahai goro,
liyo hai āṃkhī khola |
koī kahai ghara meṃ, koī kahai bana meṃ,
rādhā ke saṅga kilola |
mīrā ke prabhu giradhara nāgara,
āvata prema ke mola ||

> I have made Kṛṣṇa mine,
> I have bought him out:
> you'll say, friend, hush!
> don't bruit it about,
> but I'll shout it
> from the housetops.
> > Some say I got him cheap,
> > some say I've been fleeced,
> > but I've weighed it in the scales
> > and it's a bargain for keeps:
> Some say he's dark
> some say he's fair,
> friend, I've chosen him
> with great care
> and with eyes open.
> Some say I went
> to his house searching,
> some say I found him and Rādhā[26]
> in the woods, sporting.
> > But my Giradhara
> > is not bought with gold,
> > with all the world's wealth
> > one can't even go nigh him;
> > but to the devoted heart
> > he is sold;
> > it's only love, friend,
> > that can buy him.

19. *rāma nāma rasa pījai manuāṃ,*
    rāma nāma rasa pījai |
    taja susaṅga satasaṅga baiṭha nita,
    hari-caracā suna lījai |
    kāma krodha mada lobha moha kūṃ,

citta se bahāye dījai |
mīrā ke prabhu giradhara nāgara
vāhī ke ranga bhījai ||

> Chant the name of Rāma,
> chant it night and day,
> move with the devout
> all ears to his deeds,
> purge your mind; drive out
> pride, rage, desire and greed.
>> My Lord is Giradhara,
>> and in his love
>> my heart is ever steeped.

20. *hari mere jīvana prāṇa adhara |*
aura āsiro nahīm na tuma bina,
tīnūm loka mamjhāra |
tuma bina mohīm jaga na suhāvai,
nirakhyau saba samsāra |
mīrā kahe maim dāsī bāvarī,
lījyo neka nihāra ||

> You're my life, my soul,
> in the three worlds I see[27]
> none but you Lord Hari[28]
> who is my support:
> I'm swept helplessly
> onward in life's flow
> as a floundering boat.
>> I have scanned the earth,
>> shorn of you it seems
>> but an empty dream
>> loveless, meaningless.
> I am your bondmaid
> hungering for your sight,
> bless me with your grace,
> make my burden light.

21. *amkhiyāma tarasāma darasana pyāsī |*
maga jovata dina bītā sajanī,
naina paḍyā dukharasī |
ḍārā baiṭhi koyala bole,

bola sunyā rī gāsī |
karavā bola ḍoka jana bole,
karata hamārī hāṁsī |
mīrā hari ke hātha bikānī,
janama janama kī dāsī ||

> I only have eyes, friend,
> for Kṛṣṇa, my Loved One,
> day after day
> I pine away,
> believing each moment, he'll come.
>> When the cuckoo coos
>> it's as though a dart
>> had pierced my heart
>> through and through.
> My elders deride me
> some of them chide me
> others revile me;
> but I am sold to Kṛṣṇa,
> I'm his slave.
>> I have pledged my love to him
>> life after life
>> and I am united
>> with him always.

22. *mhaṁ giradhara āgāṁ nācyā rī |*
    nāca nāca mahāṁ rasika rijhāvāṁ,
    prīta purātana sāṁcyāṁ rī |
    syāma prīta to bāṁdhi ghuṁgharayāṁ,
    mohana mhāro sāṁcyāṁ rī |
    loka lāja kularā marajyādāṁ
    jagamāṁ neka na rakhyāṁ rī |
    prītama pala chaba nā bisarāvāṁ,
    mīrā hari raṁga rācyāṁ rī ||

> *What Mīrā said to her companion*
> I will dance before Giradhara,
> I will dance before him,
> thus I'll test
> the genuineness
> of my old love for him.[29]

I'll wear on my feet
a band of jingle-bells,
friend, my heart tells me
that his love is guileless.
Family honour, words of scorn?
I care not for these one jot,
for my Kṛṣṇa's bewitching form
is etched forever on my heart.

23. *ālī rī more nainana bāṇa paṛī |*
citta caṛhī mere mādhurī mūrata,
ura bica āna aṛī |
kaba kī ṭhāṛhī pantha nihārūṁ
apane bhavana khaṛī |
kaise prāṇa piyā binu rākhūṁ
jīvana mūla jaṛī |
mīrā giradhara hātha bikanī,
loga kahaiṁ bigaṛī |

> *What Mīrā said to her companion*
> Friend, my eyes are wedded
> to my charming Lover,
> his form is embedded
> in my heart forever
>> I have waited without end
>> for him, at my door;
>> how can I live, friend,
>> without him? he's the light
>> of my soul,
>> like the Himalayan herb
>> which revives life
>> when life's past hope.[30]
> Let busybodies say
> what they say,
> Kṛṣṇa is in my heart always
> I have surrendered to my Lover
> and now I am his slave.

24. *he mā baṛī baṛī aṁkhiyana vāro,*
sāṁvaro mo tana herata haṁsike |
bhauṁha kamāna bāna bāṁke locana,

mārata hiyare kasike |
jatana karoṁ antara likhi bāṁdhoṁ,
okhada lāūṁ ghaṁsike |
jyoṁ tokoṁ kachu aura bithā ho,
nāhina mero basike |
kauna jatana karo morī ālī,
candana lāūṁ ghasike |
antara mantara jādū tonā,
mādhuri mūrata basike |
sāṁvarī sūrata āna milāvo,
ṭhāṛhī rahuṁ maiṁ haṁsike |
rejā rejā bhayau karejā,
andara dekho dhaṁsike |
mīrā to giridhara bina dekhe
kaise rahe ghara basike ||

> *What Mīrā said to her companion*
> Friend, my large-eyed Lover
> with roving eyes
> looks me all over
> shamelessly, and smiles.
> > His eyebrows are bows
> > his lovely eyes darts
> > with which he pierces
> > deep, my heart.

> *What Mīrā's companion said to her*
> Shall I bring you an amulet
> to counter his spell,
> or grind some herb
> to make you well?
> but if love ails you
> friend, there's no help.

> *What Mīrā said to her companion*
> I'm at my wits end
> I've tried all ways,
> spells, charms, talismans
> and sandalwood-paste:
> nothing works, dear friend,
> my lovely Lover
> stays away

and my heart is rent:
just peer inside it and see
how shattered it is, friend,
his coming is the only way
by which my pain will end.
>Without him I'm lonely
>my home gives no relief,
>but if you bring him to me
>I'll laugh away my grief.

25. *thāro rūpa dekhyāṁ aṭakī |*
kula kuṭumba sajana sakala
bāra bāra haṭakī |
bisarcāṁna lagana lāgāṁ
mora mugaṭa baṭakī |
mharo mana magana syāma
loka kahyāṁ bhaṭakī |
mīrā prabhu saraṇa gahyāṁ
jānyā ghaṭa ghaṭa kī ||

>I'm stuck on Kṛṣṇa;
>my people frown,
>but I adore
>his peacock-feathered crown,
>his endearing prankishness;—
>they make me restless
>for him.
>>People say I've strayed
>>from the rightful path;
>>ah! no, I pay
>>obeisance to that Lord
>>who is the All-knowing
>>and dwells in every heart.

26. *ālo sahelyā ralī karāṁ he,*
para ghara gavana nivāri |
jhūṭhā māṇika motiyā rī,
jhūṭhī jagamaga joti |
jhūṭhā abhūṣaṇā rī,
sāṁcā piyajī kī poti |
jhūṭhā pāṭa paṭambarā re,

jhūṭhā dikhaṇī cīra,
sāṁcī piyajī kī gūdaṛī
jāme niramala rahe sarīra |
chappana bhoga buhāi de he,
ina bhogani meṁ dāga |
lūṇa alūṇom hī bhalo he
apane piyajī ko sāga |
dekhi virānai nivāṁna kūṁ he
kyūṁ upajāvai khīja |
kālara apane hi bhalo he,
jāmeṁ nipajai cīja |
chaila birāṇo lākh ko he
apane kāja na hoi |
tāke saṅga sīdhāratāṁ he,
bhalā na kahasī koi |
vara hīṇom apanoṁ bhalo he,
korhī kuṣṭī koi |
jāke saṅga sīdhāratāṁ hai,
bhalā kahai saba loi |
abināsī sūṁ bālavāṁ he,
jinasūṁ sāṁcī prīta |
mīrā kūṁ prabhu milyā he,
ehī bhagati kī rīta ||

What Mīrā said to her companions
Let us revel
in our own house,
why seek another's?
The world's treasure
is valueless
its glitter false.
    All adornments fade
    before my Love's flower-garland;
    his tattered clothes
    attract me more
    than silken garments.[31]
His simple food, e'en though unsalted
is tastier than a luxurious meal;
why be envious
of another's fertile field?

be happy with what yours will yield
what if it's fallow?
>Do not woo
>bewitching girls
>they will leave you
>in the lurch.
>Stay happy with your husband
>e'en though a leper and diseased,
>he'll ever be your support
>and all the people will extol
>your fidelity.[32]
I have won the grace
of the Infinite Being
and, friends, that's all
that devotion means.

27. *sāṁvarā nanda nandana, dīṭha paḍyāṁ māī |*
ḍāryaṁ saba loka lāja
sudha budha bisarāī |
mora candramā kirīṭa,
muguṭa chaba sohāī |
kesaru rī tilaka bhāla,
locana sukhadāī |
kuṇḍala jhalakāṁ kapola,
alakāṁ laharāī |
mīnā taja saravara jyoṁ
makara milana dhāī |
naṭavara prabhu bheṣa dharyau,
rūpa jaga lobhāī |
giradhara prabhu anga anga
mīrā bali jāī |

>*What Mīrā said to her companion*
>I'm stuck on Kṛṣṇa
>I've lost my heart to him.
>>Tongues keep tattling
>>people prattling;
>>let them:
>I adore
>>his splendid peacock-feathered crown,
>>his waving tresses tumbling down;

on his brow the *tilaka* mark,
eyes delighting, deep and dark;
earrings flashing on his cheeks
as though the fish hastens to meet
the alligator who keeps
the House of Capricorn.[33]
Friend, I long
for my Lord, Kṛṣṇa,
who has incarnated
in human form,
and captivated
all those who see him.

28. *nainā lobhī re behuri sake nahī āya |*
roma roma nakha śikha saba nirakhata,
lalaki rahai lalacāya |
maiṁ ṭhāṛhī gṛha āpane rī,
mohana nikase āya |
badana canda parakāsata helī,
manda manda musakāya |
loga kuṭumbī barajahiṁ,
mānata para hātha gal bikāya |
bhalī kaho koi burī kaho,
maiṁ saba laī sīsa caṛhāya |
mīrā ke prabhu giradhara ke bina
pala bhara rahyau na jāya ||

To feast upon his loveliness
I looked Kṛṣṇa in the eye
and now I can't take my eyes off him,
friend, they're restless for his sight,
for it ever yearning.
    I was at my door
    when he came my way,
    his moon-like face shining,
    he smiled and went away
    and left me ever pining.
My people may say what they say,
I've bartered away myself to Kṛṣṇa,
I'll willingly take both the blame and the praise,
but I can't live a moment without him.

29. *aiso prabhu jāna na dījai ho |*
tana mana dhana kari vāraṇai,
hiradai dhara lījai ho |
āva sakhī mukha dekhiye,
nainā rasa pījai ho
jiha jiha vidhi rījhai hari,
soī vidhi kījai ho |
sundara syāma suhāvaṇā,
mukha dekhyaṁ jījai ho |
mīrā ke prabhu rāmajī,
baṛa bhāgaṇa rījhe ho ||

> Do not let the Lord pass
> without an offering,
> give him your wealth, mind, life,
> everything;
> keep him in your heart.
>> See the splendour of his face
>> and his glorious majesty,
>> do all that will win his grace,
>> seek devotion at his feet.
> Kṛṣṇa is my Beloved
> whom I'm ever seeking;
> he is blessed indeed
> who can reach him.[34]

30. *mīrā lāgo ranga harī,*
aurana aṁṭaka parī |
cūṛo mhāṁre tilaka aru mālā,
sīla barata siṁgāro |
aura siṁgāra mhaṁre dāya na āvai,
yoṁ gura gyāna hamāro |
koī nindo koī bindo mheṁ to
guṇa govinda kā gāsyaṁ |
jiṇa māraga mhāṁra sādha padhārai,
uṇa māraga mheṁ jāsyaṁ |
corī na karasyaṁ jiva na satāsyaṁ,
kāṁī karasī mhāro koī |
gaja se utara ke khara nahiṁ caṛhasyaṁ,
ye to bāta na hoī ||

Kṛṣṇa alone is my Beloved,
none other.
        Bangles on my wrists
        on my brow a *tilaka*-mark
        a rosary in my hand
        and purifying fasts:
        I'm content with these,
        they're my only adornments,
        for others I don't care:
        my guru says 'Mīrā,
        you're right there.'
I do not steal
nor harm any creature,
therefore I go about
without fear.
        Worldly pleasures?
        they're trash.
        If after tasting Kṛṣṇa-love
        one still craves for them,
        it's like declining to mount an elephant
        and riding an ass!

31. *māī mhāṇe supaṇā māṁ paraṇyāṁ dīnānātha |*
chappaṇa koṭāṁ janāma padhāryāṁ
dūlho siri brajanātha |
supaṇa māṁ toraṇa bāṁdhyārī
supaṇāmāṁ gahyā hātha |
supaṇa māṁ mhāre paraṇa gayā
pāyāṁ acala sohāga |
mīrā rī giradhara milyārī,
puraba jaṇama rī bhāga ||

    Friend, I dreamt I married Kṛṣṇa;
    there were five hundred and sixty million men
    in the marriage procession,
    and Kṛṣṇa at its head;
    festoons decked
    the gay pavilion.[35]
        He took my hand in his
        making me his bride.
    It's only because of my good works, friend,

in past lives
that I could even in a dream
become Kṛṣṇa's wife.

32. *barajī rī mhāṁ syāma binā na rahyā |*
sādhāṁ saṅgata hari sukha pāsyūṁ
jagasūṁ dūra rahyā |
tana mana mhārāṁ jāvāṁ jāsyāṁ
mhāre sīkha lahyā |
mana mhāro lagyāṁ giradhārī
jagarā bola sahyā |
mīrā ke prabhu hari avināsī,
thārī saraṇa gahyā ||

> Men ask me to keep away
> from Kṛṣṇa, but how can I?
> he's my love, my life.
>> I delight
>> in the assembly of sadhus,
>> there I chant Kṛṣṇa's name
>> undisturbed;
>> therefore I turn away
>> from the world.
>> I've surrendered to him
>> body, mind and wealth
>> and for his sake
>> I cheerfully bear
>> all taunts and slurs
> My Lord is the Imperishable Hari
> and I've cast myself
> at his feet.

33. *nahiṁ sukha bhāvai thāṁro desalaṛo raṁgarūṛo |*
thāṁre desāṁ meṁ rāṇā sadhu nahiṁ chai,
loga basai saba kūṛo |
ghaṇā gāṁṭhī rāṇā hama saba tyāgā,
tyāgyo kara ro cūṛo |
kājala ṭīkī hama saba tyāgā,
tyāgyo chai bāṁdhana jūṛo |
mīrā ke prabhu giradhara nāgara
bara pāyo chai pūro ||

What Mīrā said to the Rāṇā (her brother-in-law)
Keep your kingdom to yourself
O Rāṇā, it does not attract me
for it is bereft of holy men,
only the worldly-minded live there
    and all they treasure
    is sensual pleasures
    there's nothing but dirt in their minds,
    O Rāṇā, I have renounced
    all wealth and adornments,
    there's no *ṭīkā* on my forehead[36]
    no lamp-black in my eyes
    and my hair remains unbraided.
What need have I to deck
my body with such trinklets,
O Rāṇā, when I have wed
Kṛṣṇa, Master of the worlds?

34. *acche mīṭhe cākha cākha*
    bera lāī bhīlaṇī |
    aisī kahā acāravatī
    rūpa nahīm eka ratī;
    nīce kula ochī jāta,
    ati hī kucīlaṇī |
    jūṭhe phala līnhem rāma
    prema kī pratīta jāṇi |
    ūmca nīca jāne nahīm,
    rasa kī rasīlaṇī |
    aisī kahā veda paṛhī,
    china mem vimana caṛhī |
    hari jī sūm bāmdhyo hetu
    baikuṇṭha mem jhūlaṇī |
    dāsa mīrā tarai soi
    aisī prīta karai joi |
    patita-pāvana prabhu
    gokula ahīraṇī ||

What Mīrā said to her companion
The tribal woman[37]
offered Rāma plums
biting each one

to see if it was sweet!
    Of low caste,
    low clan,
    unrefined, ignorant
    she.
    Yet Rāma ate them
    for they were given with love,
    yes, he ate those leftovers,
    he.
To God are alike
high and low,
he delights
in those who give him
love:
    and so that woman
    went to heaven;
    for God is kind
    to those who love him
    and forgives them
    all their sins.
In my past life
I was a *gopī,*[38]
so, friend, surely
he will redeem me.

35. *bidha bidhāna rī nyāri santo*
    bidha bidhāna rī nyārī |
    baṛe baṛe nayana diye maraghana kūṁ
    bana bana phirata ughārī re |
    ujjavala barana dīnī bagalana kūṁ
    koyala kara dīnī kālī re |
    aura nadiyana jala niramala kīno,
    samudara kara dīnī khārī re |
    mūrakha kū tuma rāja diyata ho
    paṇḍita phirata bhikārī re |
    mīrā ke prabhu giradhara nāgara
    rāṇāṁ bhagata saṁghārī re ||

    What Mīrā said to her companion
    God's ways are strange indeed,
    he gave the deer large eyes

but made him hide
in the forest depths
so that their loveliness
is unrevealed.
  He made the wily fish-preying heron
  dazzling white,
  and the sweet-voiced cuckoo
  black as night!
He made the river-waters sweet
and the sea-water salt;
he made fools kings
and caused wise men
to beg from door to door![39]
  Is it not strange friend,
  that God heaps sorrows
  on his devotees
  just to test them?

36. *yā braj meṁ kachu dekhyo rī ṭonā |*
  le maṭukī sira cali gujariyā,
  āge mile bābā nandajī ke chonā |
  dadhi ko nāma bisari gayo pyārī
  'lai lehu rī kou syāma salonā |
  bindrābana kī kunja galina meṁ
  āṁkha lagāya gayo manamohanā |
  mīrā ke prabhu giradhara nāgara
  sundara syāma sughara rasa lonā ||

 What Mīrā said to her companion
 Ah! friend, what wizardry!
 A girl of Braja
 pot on head[40]
 calling out
  'buy my curd,
  buy my curd'.
  Kṛṣṇa passed by;
  bewitched by him
  she began to call
  'buy lovely Kṛṣṇa!
  buy lovely Kṛṣṇa!'
 Thus in Vṛndāvana's shady lanes

ravishing Kṛṣṇa
left that girl lovelorn.
    I have lost my heart
    to that same
    charming Dark Lord
    I am caught forever
    in the net of his love.

37. *mhāre ghara āo prītama pyārā,*
    tuma bina saba jaga khārā |
    tana mana dhana saba bheṁṭa dharūṁgī,
    bhajana karūṁgī tumhārā |
    tuma guṇavanta su sāhiba kahiye,
    momeṁ auguṇa sārā |
    maiṁ niguṇī kachu guṇa nahiṁ jānūṁ,
    tuma ho bagasaṇahāra |
    mīrā kahai prabhu kaba re miloge,
    tuma bina naina dukhārā ||

    Come to me, Lover,
    without you the world seems joyless,
    take all I have
    body, soul—everything;
    I will keep chanting your name for ever.
        All virtues are in you,
        all wickedness in me:
        you are all goodness
        I'm all evil;
        but I know you are merciful
        and will forgive all my sins.
    When will you come, Kṛṣṇa Beloved?
    I am waiting, waiting,
    my eyes pine for your sight
    and my heart is aching.

38. *sunī ho maiṁ hari āvaṁgā āja |*
    mahala caṛha-caṛha jōūṁ merī sajanī
    kaba āvaiṁ maharāja |
    dādura mora papihā bolai,
    koyala madhura sāja |
    umaṁgyau indra chauṁ disi barasai,

dāmaṇi choṛī lāja |
dharatī rūpa nava nava dhariya,
indra milaṇa kai kāja |
mīrā ke prabhu hari avināsī,
vega milo maharāja ||

> *What Mīrā said to her companion*
> I hear Kṛṣṇa's coming
> today.
> I climb the palace roof
> looking out for him.
>> toads and peacocks
>> are drunk with glee
>> the cuckoo and *papīhā*[41]
>> sing melodiously:
> the rumbling clouds gather
> and pour on the parched earth:
> the naked Lightning
> rushes shamelessly
> to make love to the Clouds:
> the bare Earth
> adorns herself
> and puts on a new dress,
> as though to meet Indra.[42]
>> Kṛṣṇa, Lover,
>> hasten, I beseech you,
>> delay no longer
>> I'm dying to meet you.

39. *covata hī palakā meṁ maiṁ to,*
    palaka lagī pala meṁ piva āye |
    maiṁ jo uṭhī prabhu ādara deṇa kūṁ,
    jāga paṛī piva ḍhūṁḍha na pāye |
    aura sakhī piva soi gamāye,
    maiṁ ju sakhī piva jāgi gamāye
    mīrā ke prabhu giradhara nāgara,
    saba sukha hoya syāma ghara āye ||

> Shut in sleep
> my eyes find my Lover,
> when they open
> they lose him.

> Others miss lovemaking
> when sleeping,
> I miss it by
> waking.
> Come home and please me
> Kṛṣṇa Beloved,
> do not now
> keep me waiting.

40. *papaiyā re piva kī vāṇī na bola |*
suni pāvelī biṛahaṇī re,
thāṁrī ḍārelī pāṁkha marora |
coṁca kaṭāūṁ papaiyā re,
ūpara kalora lūṇa |
piva merā maiṁ piva kī re,
tū piva kahai su kūṇa |
thārā sabada suhāvaṇā re
jo piva melā āja |
coṁca maṁrhāūṁ thārī sovanī re,
tū mere siratāja |
prītama kūṁ patiyāṁ likhūṁ re,
kāgā tū le jāya |
jāi prītama jāsūṁ yūṁ kahai re,
thāṁrī virahaṇa dhāna na khāya |
mīrā dāsī byākula re,
piva-piva karata bihāya |
bega milau prabhu antarajāmī,
tuma bina rahyau na jāya ||

> *What Mīrā said to the papīhā*
> Wretched bird,
> calling *pi, pi*[43]
> to your mate:
>> don't you know
>> my Beloved's away
>> and your voice
>> wrings my heart?
> Cease:
> or I'll have your wings taken apart,
> your beak cut off
> and sprinkled with black salt

so that you'll hop about
mad with pain!
    Who are you
    to call out to my Lover,
    don't you know
    he's mine and I'm his,
    forever?
But if your plaintive notes
can bring my Lover back,
darling bird! I'll have
your beak gilded with gold!

Mīrā goes on to say to the crow
O crow, I'll give you a letter
for my Lover,
hold it in your beak
and swiftly fly:
tell him I've forsaken
all food, and I'm wasting,
and if he does not hasten
to me, I'll die.
    Go tell my Giradhara,
    the All-knowing One,
    I can live no longer
    if he does not come.

41. *koī kahiyau re prabhu āvana kī |*
āvana kī manabhāvana kī |
āpa na āvai likha nahiṁ bhejai,
bāṇa parī lalacāvana kī |
ye doi naina kahyau nahiṁ mānai,
nadiyāṁ bahai jaise sāvana kī |
kahā karūṁ kachu basa nahiṁ merau,
pāṁkha nahiṁ ura jāvana kī |
mīrā kahai prabhu kaba re miloge,
ceri bhaī hūṁ tere dāṁvana kī ||

    Tell me someone
    will Kṛṣṇa come
    to delight me?
        He does as he pleases,
        he won't even write to me,

O what a teaser he is!
I can't hold back my tears
they keep arising ever
flowing copiously
as Sāvana's flooded rivers.[44]
If I had wings
I'd fly to him.
When will you come, Kṛṣṇa?
you are my life, my hope,
O Beloved, you are
my life's only support.

42. *karama gata ṭāre nahiṁ ṭarai* |
satavādī haricaṁd-se rājā (so to)
ḍoma ghara nīra bharai |
pāṁca pāṁḍu rī rānī dropadī
hāḍa himālai garai |
jagya kiyo balī lena indrāsaṇa,
so pātāla dharai |
mīrā ke prabhu giradhara nāgara,
bikha se amṛta karai ||

No one can escape
destiny;
as God wills
so will it be.[45]
The truthful
king Hariścandra
had to fill water from the well
of an outcaste:[46]
queen Draupadī
wife of the Pāṇḍavas
died miserably
on the Himalayas:[47]
king Bali,
who performed a *yajña,*
to take Indra's place
in heaven;
losing all
had to be content
with the nether regions.[48]

>   Mīrā's Lord is Giradhara
>   who turned
>   poison
>   into nectar.[49]

43. *jogiyā sūm prīta kiyā dukha hoya |*
    prīta kiyā sukha nā morī sajanī,
    jogī mīmta na koya |
    rāta-divasa kala nāhim parata hai,
    tuma miliyām bina moya |
    aisī sūrata yā jaga māhīm,
    pheri na dekhī soya |
    mīrā ke prabhu kabare miloge,
    miliyām ānamda hoya |

>   Yogi Lover,
>   you bring me
>   nothing but sorrow.
>   Today you're with me
>   you will go away
>   leaving me lonesome
>   tomorrow.
>   What's the good of
>   loving a yogi?
>   he brings only grief
>   and he cares for none;
>   I pine night and day
>   to see his matchless face,
>   but he does not come.
>   Come, come Lover,
>   I'm starved
>   of your sight;
>   come and fill
>   my sorrowing heart
>   with delight.

44. *sīsodyau rūṭhyo to mhāmro kaim karalesī |*
    mhem to guṇa govinda kā gāsyām, ho māī
    rāṇo jī ruṭhyo vāro deśa rakhāsī |
    hari rūṭhyā kumhalasyām, ho māī
    loka lāja kī kāṇa na mānūm |

nirabhai nisāna ghūrāsyāṁa, ho māī
syāma nāma kā jhāṁjha calāsyāṁ |
bhavasāgara tara jāsyāṁ, ho māī
mīra saraṇa saṁvala giradhara kī |
caraṇa kaṁvala lapaṭāṁsyāṁ, ho māī ||

> *What Mīrā said to her companion*
> What if the Rāṇā is displeased
> and banishes me from his domain?
> friend, I will not cease
> to chant Kṛṣṇa's name.
>> The Rāṇā can only make me
>> leave his kingdom,
>> but if Kṛṣṇa forsakes me
>> I'll be undone;
>> I'll fade away
>> as a wilted creeper,
>> for my mainstay
>> is my Giradhara.
> I care not, friend,
> for wagging tongues,
> I will fearlessly beat
> the drum of devotion.
>> I will clap the cymbals
>> of Kṛṣṇa-love
>> they will take me across
>> the treacherous ocean
>> of deaths and rebirths.
> My Dark Lord
> is the Almighty.
> 'Tis his grace I seek;
> he will save me
> from all perils,
> I will clasp his feet.[50]

45. *ho gaye syāma duija ke candā |*
madhubana jāya rahe madhubaniyā
hama para ḍāro prema ko phandā |
mīrā ke prabhu giradhara nāgara,
aba to neha paro kachu mandā ||

Kṛṣṇa has gone away to Mathurā,[51]
like the new moon
vanished soon,
he's now rarely seen.[52]
He left us
caught
in love's snare,
but he doesn't care.
> Giradhara is my Lord
> but his love has waned
> and he remains
> indifferent now.

46. *candā jāyagā sūraja jāyagā,*
    jāyagī dharaṇa akāsī |
    pavana pānī donūṁ hī jāyaṁge,
    aṭala rahai abināsī |
    aura sakhī mada pī-pī mātī,
    maiṁ bina piyāṁ hī mātī |
    prema bhaṭhī ko maiṁ mada pīyo,
    chakī phirūṁ dina-rātī |
    surata nirata ko divalo joyo,
    manasā kī kara lī bātī |
    agama ghāṇi ko tela siṁcāyo,
    bāla rahī dina-rātī |
    jaūṁnī pīhariye jaūṁnī sāsariye
    harisūṁ saina lagāti |
    mīrā ke prabhu giradhara nāgara,
    hari caraṇā cita lātī ||

Everything perishes,
sun, moon, earth, sky,
water, wind,—
everything.
> Only the One
> Indestructible
> remains.
Others get drunk on
distilled wine,
in love's still
I distil mine;

day and night
I'm drunk on it
in my Lover's
love, ever sunk.
          Wrapt in God
          I meditate,
          my lamp's
          his sacred name;
          in it my mind
          as wick I place
          and feed its light
          with oil that's made
          from knowledge's oil-press,
          and its flame
          keep burning
          day and night.
I'll not remain
in my mother's home,
I'll stay
with Kṛṣṇa alone;
          he's my Husband
          and my Lover,
          and my mind is
          at his feet forever.

47. *piyā mohi darasaṇa dījai ho* |
bera-bera maiṁ ṭera hūṁ
yā kirapā kījai ho |
jeṭha mahīne jala binā,
panchī dukha hoī ho
mora asaṛhāṁ kuralahe,
ghana cātaga soī ho |
sāvaṇa meṁ jhaṛa lāgiyo,
sakhi tījāṁ khelai ho |
bhādaravai nadiyāṁ bahaiṁ
dūrī jina melai ho |
sīpa svāti hī jhelatī,
āsojāṁ soī ho |
deva kātiga pujahe,
mere tuma hoi ho |

saṅgasara ṭhaṇḍa bahotū paṛai,
mohi begi samhālo ho |
posa mahīṁ pālā ghaṇā
abahī tuma nhāloho |
mahā mahīṁ basanta pañcamī,
phāgāṁ saba gāvai ho |
phāguna phāgāṁ khelahaiṁ,
banarāya jarāvai ho |
caita citta meṁ ūpajī,
darasaṇa tuma dījai ho |
baisākh banarāi phūlavai,
koila kuralījai ho |
kāga uṛāvata dina gayā,
būjhūṁ paṇḍita josī ho |
mīrā birahaṇa vyakulī
darasaṇa kada hosī ho ||

Come, Lover,
come:
>   In the Jeṭha month
>   water-starved birds with parched throats
>   gasp for breath.

In Asāṛha
the *cātakas* and peacocks[53]
call for rain.
>   In Sāvaṇa
>   it's drizzle drizzle
>   all the day
>   and girls celebrate
>   the Tīja festival.[54]

Don't stay away
in Bhādoṁ, Lover,
the flooded rivers
are uncrossable then.
>   In Kārtika women
>   worship gods,
>   but why need I
>   when Kṛṣṇa is my Lord?

Bitter cold Agahana
and frosty Pūṣa

bring no relief,
hasten, Lover
and end my grief.
>Māgha brings
>*phāga* songs[55]
>and the Basanta-pañcamī.[56]
With coloured powders and sprays
revellers celebrate
Holī in Phāguna.[57]
With spring close,
Lover,
my heart longs for you
all the more.
>In Caitra
>I can no longer bear
>parting's sting.
Baisākha leaves me more distraught;
blossoms blooming
bare brown branches
leaves renewing,
bright spring slaying
winter's frost.
>The koel calls
>*cu-cu;*
>the cawing of crows
>fills me with hope,[58]
>I've asked astrologers and pundits
>but all in vain.
You do not come
nor send a message,
my lonely heart
is agitated,
my eyes hunger for you;
when will you satiate them
with your sight,
O Lover,
when?[59]

48. *pyāre darasana dījyo āye* |
   tuma bina rahyau na jāya ||

jala bina kamala, canda bina rajanī,
aise tuma dekhyāṁ bina sajanī |
ākula-vyākula phirūṁ raina dina,
biraha kalejo khāye |
divasa na bhūkha, nīṁda nahiṁ rainā,
mukha sūṁ kahata na āvai bainā |
kahā kahūṁ kachu kahata na āvai,
milakara tapata bujhāi |
kyūṁ tarasāvo antarajāmī,
āye milo kirapā kara swāmī |
mīrā dāsī janama-janama kī,
paṛungī tumhāre pāi ||

> Lover, come,
> without you I am
>   as the lotus without water,
>   night without the moon.
> Night and day
> I wander restlessly
> parting's barb
> in my heart
> embedded.
>   Stung by grief
>   I cannot eat
>   and all the night
>   I know no sleep.
> Words?
> ah! how can they speak out
> the grief
> that's buried deep?
>   Come Lover,
>   only you
>   can put out the fire that burns me;
>   Knower of hearts
>   why do you torment me?
>   I'm your slave
>   life after life,
>   I will clasp
>   Your hallowed feet.

49. *dāṛi gayo manamohana pāsī |*

āṁbā ki ḍāla koyala ika bolai,
mero maraṇa aru jaga kare hāṁsī |
biraha kī mārī maiṁ bana bana ḍolūṁ,
praṇa tajūm karavata lyūṁ kāsī |
mīrā ke prabhu hari abināsī,
tuma mere ṭhākura maiṁ terī dāsī ||

> You
> placed the noose of parting
> round my neck
> Lover,
> and went away.
> > The koel calls
> > *cu-cu*
> > breaking my heart,
> > the world laughs
> > at me.
> I wander in the woods
> wild with grief.
> If you do not come
> I'll die
> in holy Kāśī.[60]
> > O Eternal Being
> > you are my Master,
> > your slave
> > I.

50. *ko birahinī ko dukha jāṁnai ho |*
    jā ghaṭā birahā soi lakhihai,
    kai koī harijana mānai ho |
    rogi antara baida basata hai,
    baida hī okhada jāṁṇai ho |
    biraha darada uri antari māṁhī
    hari bini saba sukha kāṁnai ho |
    dugadhā āraṇa phirai dukhārī
    surata basī suta māṁnai ho |
    cātaga svāti būṁda mana māṁhī,
    pīla ukalāṁne ho |
    saba jaga kūṛo kaṇṭaka duniyā,
    darada na koī pichānai ho |
    mīrā ke pati rameyā,

dujo nahiṁ koi chāṇai ho ||

> Who can know
> parting's anguish?
> > Only he who is heartbroken,
> > or he who is
> > God's devotee.
> Only the doctor
> knows the disease
> only he
> can cure it.
> > So long as Kṛṣṇa
> > is not with me
> > all the world's pleasures
> > are trash.
> The milch cow
> grazes in the woods
> but her mind is
> with her calf.
> > The *cātaka*[61]
> > restless for the *svāti* rain
> > scans the sky
> > for clouds.
> So too, Kṛṣṇa,
> I pine for you,
> for you, Lover,
> far away.
> > All existence is
> > worldly bondage
> > no one can know
> > of my grief:
> Kṛṣṇa is my Darling Lover
> and for me
> there's none but he.

51. *paga ghuṁgharū bāṁdha mīrā nācī re|*
    maiṁ to mere nārāyaṇa kī,
    āpahī ho gaī dāsī re|
    loga kahaiṁ mīrā bhaī bāvarī,
    nyāta kahai kulanāsī re|
    viṣa kā pyālā rāṇājī bhejyā,

pīvata mīrā hāṁsī re |
mīrā ke prabhu giradhara nāgara,
sahaja milā avināsī re |

> With a band of jingling bells
> tied to my ankles
> I dance away;
> I have pledged
> my life to God.
>> She is moonstruck
>> people say
>> and my relations say
>> she brings us disgrace.
> The Rāṇā sent me
> a cup of poison[62]
> I drank it off
> and laughed and laughed!
>> My Lord is Giradhara,
>> I'm his slave;
>> I have won
>> effortlessly
>> that Eternal Being's
>> grace.

52. *syāma milana ke kāja sakhī,*
mere ārati ura meṁ jāgī rī |
talaphata-talaphata kala na parata hai,
biraha bāṇa ura lāgī rī |
nisa-dina pantha nihārūṁ piva ko,
palaka na pala bhari lāgī rī |
pīva-pīva maiṁ raṭūṁ rāta-dina,
dūjī sudha-budha bhāgī rī |
biraha bhujanga mero ḍasyo hai kalejau,
lahari halāhala jāgī rī |
merī ārati meṭi guṁsāī,
āyi milau mohiṁ sāgī rī |
mīrā vyākula ati akulāṇī,
piyā kī umanga ati lāgī rī ||

> Wounded
> with affliction's shaft

my heart is restless;
I long for Kṛṣṇa
sleeping not a wink,
his name on my lips
nightlong.
    My eyes are glued to the drive
    expecting his coming:
    parting's agony
    is like a serpent-bite,
    its poison swiftly
    spreading.
I'm restless for you, Lover,
come and end my grief,
without you my agony
can find no relief.

53. *ramaiyā bina yau jivaro dukha pāvai,*
    kaho kuṇa dhīra baṁdhāvai |
    yā saṁsāra kubudha ko bhāṁḍo,
    sādha-saṅgati nahīṁ bhāvai |
    rāma nāma kī nindā ṭhāṇai,
    karama-hī-karama kumāvai |
    rāma nāma bina mukuti na pāvai |
    phira caurāsī jāvai |
    sādha-saṅgati kabahūṁ na jāvai,
    mūrakha janama gaṁvāvai |
    mīrā prabhu giradhara ke saraṇe,
    jīva parama pada pāvai ||

The heart's grief
can't find relief
without the love of Rāma.
    This world is
    a cauldron of ills
    it does not honour saints.
    can men ever attain
    emancipation
    if they revile Rāma's name?
They're reborn again and again
upon this grief-filled earth.
These vile men are bound forever

to the wheel of eighty-four lakh births.[63]
    To the saints
these fools never go,
their lives a vain endeavour;
says Mīrā, take refuge in Rāma
or you won't get *mokṣa* ever.[64]

54. *tosoṁ lāgyau neha re*
pyāre nāgara nanda kumāra |
murali tori mana haryau,
bisarayau ghara-vyauhāra |
jaba taiṁ śravanani dhuni pari,
ghara aṁganā na suhāya,
paradhi jyūṁ cūke nahīṁ,
mṛgī bedhi dai āya |
pāni pīra na jānai jyoṁ,
mīna taṛapha mari jāya |
rasika madhupa ke marama ko nahīṁ.
samujhata kamala subhāya |
dīpaka ko jo dayā nahīṁ,
uṛi-uṛi marata putanga,
mīrā prabhu giradhara mile,
jaise pāṇi mili gayau ranga ||

    I've lost my heart to you, Kṛṣṇa,
when the notes
of your flute
fall
on my ears,
forgotten are home, relations, courtyard—
all.
    Heartless Lover,
you are like
a hunter taking aim
at the frozen deer:
the draining water
which does not know the pain
of the fish that writhe:
the lovely lotus
cold

to the nectar-sucking bee
imprisoned inside.
You're like
the lamp that burns
unconcerned
as moths haste
to immolate
upon its flame.
Says Mīrā, Giradhara
you and I
as water and dye
are different only
in the name.

55. *darasa binu dūkhana lāgai naina |*
jaba se tuma bichure prabhu more
kabhum na pāyau caina |
sabada sunata meri chatiyām kāmpai
mīthe lāgaim baina |
biraha kathā kāsūm kahūm sajanī,
baha gaī karavata aina |
kala na parata pala hari maga jovata,
bhaī chamāsī raina |
mīrā ke prabhu kaba re miloge,
dukha metana sukha daina ||

My eyes thirst
for your sight;
ever since you left
I know no rest
your honeyed words haunt me
day and night.
Whom shall I tell
my parting's grief?
'tis as though the blade
of a sword has made
a wound that does not heal.
Love, you've left me and gone,
each dreary night seems
six month's long,

I do not know
when comes the dawn.
        O Lover, Lord,
        when will you come,
        Beloved, when,
        to end the pain
        that gnaws my heart,
        and bring me joy again?

56. *koī kachu kahe mana lāgā |*
aisī prīta lagī manamohana,
jyūm sonā mem suhāgā |
janama-janama kā soyā manuā
satagura sabda suṇa jāgā |
māta pitā suta kuṭuma kabīlā
ṭuṭa gayau jyūm tāgā |
mīrā ke prabhu giradhara nāgara,
bhāga hamārā jāgā ||

> *What Mīrā said to her companion*
> Let people say
> what they like,
> Kṛṣṇa and I
> are one, friend,
> as borax
> in gold ornaments.
>   My mind was ever
>   dark as night,
>   by my guru's grace
>   'tis now awake
>   and I have seen the light.
> All the bonds are broken
> as a severed thread—
> parents, sons, relations—
> and, O Lord Giradhara,
> in your love alone
> my restless mind finds rest.

57. *bādala dekha ḍarī ho syāma!*
maim bādala dekha ḍarī |
kālī-pīlī ghaṭā ūmmaṛī

barasyo eka gharī
jita jāūm̐ tita pāṇī pāṇī,
huī bhumi harī |
jākā piya paradesa basata hai,
bhījum̐ bahāra kharī |

> Kṛṣṇa, I'm scared
> to see the clouds gather,
> black clouds
> yellow clouds
> massed together:
> O Kṛṣṇa, I'm scared.
>> All in a moment
>> they pour and pour
>> more and more,
>> it's water, water
>> everywhere.
> The thirsty earth
> drinks in the rain,
> the withered plants
> are green again.
>> My lover is in far-off lands
>> while at my door
>> I stand alone,
>> getting soaked through and through.
> O Lord Imperishable
> make my love pure,
> I pray to you
> O Giradhara,
> make me yours.[65]

58. *mohī lāgī lagana guru-caraṇana kī* |
caraṇa binā kachuve nahim̐ bhāva,
jaga māyā saba sapanana kī |
bhau sāgara saba sūkha gayo hai,
phikara nahīm̐ mohi taranana kī |
mīrā ke prabhu giradhara nāgara
āsa vahī guru-saranana kī |

> This world is like
> a dream that's fled;

therefore I seek
my guru's feet
I delight in nothing else.
>This world is like a dried ocean,
>meaningless;
>I don't seek *mokṣa*[66]
>I only hope
>to get the love of
>Giradhara.
He's my Beloved
he's my Guru,
what have I to do with the world?

59. *maiṁ to terī saraṇa pari re*
he rāmā jyūṁ jāṇe jyūṁ tāra |
aṛasaṭha tīratha bhrama bhrama āyo,
mana nahiṁ mānī hāra |
yā jagameṁ koī nahiṁ apaṇā,
suṇiyau śravaṇa murāra |
mīrā dāsī rāma bharose
jama kā phandā nivāra ||

>I have come to you, Kṛṣṇa,[67]
>do as you wish,
>I have been all over
>seeking for you, Lover,
>still you remained hid.
>>Yet I'll persevere
>>who is mine here?
>>Who?
>>Hear me Lover, hear,
>>I have only
>>You.
>Lord, take me across
>the uncrossable sea;
>from births and rebirths
>make me free.

60. *naināṁ aṭake rūpa sūṁ,*
pala pala nahiṁ lāge |
nisi-dina cātraka ūṁcahe,

soe nahiṁ, jāge |
basana-ābhūṣaṇa saba taji
piya ke anurāge |
mohana mūrati hṛdi basī,
alabelī pāge |
mātu-pitā suta bandhuvā,
raci-paci saba bhāge |
mīna biyogī kyoṁ jie,
jaba jala tiṇa tyāge |
mīrā prabhu giradhara mile,
piya seja suhāge |
chaṭhe-chāhāra unakī parau,
je āpuna ye bhāge ||

In less than a moment
Lover, you were
imprisoned in my eyes:
every night the cuckoo calls
sleep-starved, awake I lie.
        Fancy garments,
        ornaments,
        I have foresworn:
        your love alone is that
        for which I long.
Your glorious turban
lovely face
enthrall me
and I gaze and gaze.
        For your sake
        I have forsaken
        parents, sons, relations;
        your love alone
        has awakened
        in my heart.
O Lover, you are
the life of my life,
abandoned by the water
can the fish survive?
        I'm wedded now to you
        Giradhara,[68]

O Lord Beloved, yours is
the nuptial bed:
sometimes you come
but often stay away,
such is my fate, O Lover,
what can I say?

61. *gohane gopāla phirūṁ,*
aisī āvata mana meṁ |
avalokata bārija badana,
bibasa bhaī tana meṁ |
muralī kara lukaṭa leuṁ,
pīta basana dhārūṁ |
ācho gopa bheṣa mukuṭa,
godhana ke saṁga cārūṁ |
hama bhaī gula kāma-latā,
bṛndābana rainā
pasu, panchī, marakaṭa,
munī sravana sunata baināṁ |
gurujana kī kaṭhina kāni,
kāsom rī kahie |
mīrā prabhu giridhara mili,
aisaiṁ hī rahie ||

I'd like to be with Kṛṣṇa always;
when I saw his lotus-face
my heart was lost to him.
I'll dress in yellow silk and take
in my hand a stick flute-shaped
I'll wander in the countryside
and take the cows to graze.
Vṛndāvana is my real home
where live hermits of saintly minds,
birds sing and beasts and monkeys roam;
there I'll live as a tender vine.
The elders may raise their eyebrows
but I have pledged my love to Kṛṣṇa,
and after meeting him that's how
it's best to live for him.

62. *more to mana rāma-caraṇa sukhadāī |*

jina caraṇana soṁ nikasī surasari,
saṁkara-jaṭā samāī |
jaṭa-śaṅkarī nāma dharyau hai
tribhuvana tārana āī |
jina caraṇana kī bimala pādukā,
bharata rahe lava lāī |
jo kevaṭa kahaṁ pāvana kīnho,
jaba prabhu nāva caṛhāī |
daṇḍaka-bana rāma pāvana kīnhī,
muniyana dukha miṭāī |
jo ṭhākuratihuṁ loka kau svāmī
kapaṭakuraṁga saṁga dhāī |
kapi sugrīva bandhu-bhaya byākula,
jā sira chatra dharāī |
ṛpu kau anuja vibhisaṇa bheṭyau,
mīrā kī bārī āī ||

In Lord Rāma's feet I find bliss,
those feet from which the Gaṅgā came
and was contained
in the matted hair of Śiva,[69]
with which its furious torrent was checked—
and so it's known as 'Śankara's crest':
from there it flowed onward
to purify the three worlds.[70]
Feet,
the sandals of which
Bharata placed
upon his head with love.[71]

      The sacred feet
      that Kevaṭa laved
      and was by their touch purified
      ere he took Rāma across:[72]
      the holy feet
      which sanctified
      the Daṇḍaka forest
      which they trod:
      the feet of him
      who allayed
      the grief that hermits gnawed.
   The feet of him

without compeer
who rules the world,
yet who pursued
a runaway elusive deer![73]
The feet of him
who crowned Sugrīva
when he was grieved
by his own brother.
The feet of him
who gave refuge
to Vibhīṣaṇa
whom Rāvaṇa spurned.[74]
     Says Mīrā, Lord,
     it is my turn
     now, to receive your grace.

63. *nainana baṇaja basāūṁ rī*
    mhārā sāṁvarā āvā |
    nenāṁ mhārā sāṁvarā rājyā
    ḍarati palaka na nāūṁ rī |
    mhāre hiridya meṁ basā murārī,
    pala pala darasana pauṁ rī |
    syāma milana siṁgāra sajāūṁ
    sukharī seja bichāūṁ rī |
    mīrā ke prabhu giradhara nāgara,
    bāra bāra bali jāūṁ rī ||

When my Dark Lover comes
I'll feast my eyes
on his lotus-face;
I will not let them droop
for fear I lose
its sight.
     His form dwells ever in my mind,
     not a moment passes by
     when it's not before my eyes:
     to meet him I adorn myself
     and spread
     for him the nuptial-bed.
Kṛṣṇa is my Lord
to him I have

                surrendered all that I
                possess.

64. *māī mhāṁ govinda guṇa gāsyāṁ |*
    caraṇāmṛta ro nema sakāre,
    nita uṭha darasaṇa jāsyāṁ |
    hari mandira māṁ nirata karāvāṁ,
    ghuṁgharajā ghamakāsyāṁ |
    syāma nāma ro jhāṁjha calāsyāṁ
    bhosāgara tara jāsyāṁ |
    yo saṁsāra bīraro kāṁṭo,
    gela prītama aṭakāsyāṁ |
    mīrā re prabhu giradhara nāgara,
    guṇa gāvāṁ pāsyāṁ ||

        What Mīrā said to her companion
        I will sing Kṛṣṇa's praises, friend,
        early morning I will go
        to get the curd and ghee,
        ambrosia of his holy feet.
            I will go to temple where
            his image is, and offer prayers,
            and to rhythm of cymbals
            dance
            with abandoned ecstasy.
        O Lover, why have you got
        me entangled in this world
        as one who's helplessly caught
        in a thorny berry-shrub?
            But I'll chant your name
            and free
            myself from these bonds;
            O Lord Giradhara,
            I will be
            yours eternally.

65. *mīrā magana bhaī hari ke guṇa gāye |*
    sāṁpa piṭārā rāṇā bhejyo
    mīrā hāth diyo jāya |
    nyāha dhoya jaba dekhana lāgī
    sāligarāma gaī pāya |

jahara kā pyālā rāṇā bhejyā
amṛta dīnha banāya |
nyāha dhoya jaba pīvana lāgī,
ho gaī amara aṁcāya |
sūla seja rāṇā ne bhejī,
diyo mīrā sulāya |
sāṁjha bhaī mīrā sovana lāgī
māno phūla bichāya |
mīrā ke prabhu sadā sahāī,
rākhe bidhana haṭāya |
bhajana bhāva meṁ masta ḍolatī |
giradhara paī bali jāya ||

> I love to sing the praise
> of Kṛṣṇa, my saviour,
> he rescues me always
> from all the ills here.
>> The Rāṇā sent me a basket[75]
>> with a snake inside it,
>> when I opened the lid
>> lo! it was a stone idol![76]
> He sent me a poisoned cup
> but it turned to nectar!
> I joyfully drank it up
> Kṛṣṇa is my protector.
>> He sent a bed of spikes
>> for me to sleep on,
>> but when I slept at night
>> each spike was a blossom!
> How can one harm ever
> him whom the Lord loves?
> I have surrendered
> myself to Giradhara.

66. *nandanaṁdana bilamāī, badarā ne gherī māī |*
ita ghana laraje uta ghana garaje,
camakata bijju sabāī |
umara ghumara cahuṁ disa se āye,
pavana calai puravāī |
dādura mora papīhā bolai,
koyala sabada suṇāī |

mīrā ke prabhu giradhara nāgara,
caraṇa kaṁvala cita lāī ||

> *What Mīrā said to her companion*
> Kṛṣṇa is not seen
> friend, it seems
> he has been bewitched
> by some lovely lass
> and stays there:
>> while here the clouds
>> amass
>> rushing from every side,
>> streaks of lighting
>> flash
>> across the sky:
> the easterly wind blows
> bringing cool showers
> peacocks dance, frogs croak,
> sparrow-hawks call,
> and the cuckoo's voice
> enthralls
> lovelorn hearts.
>> My Lord is Giradhara
>> whose feet I adore,
>> he is my protector
>> he is my support.

67. *badalā re tū jala bhari le āyau* |
choṭī-choṭī būṁdana barasana lāgyo,
koyala sabada sunāyau |
gājal-bājai pavana madhuriyā,
ambara badarā chāyau |
seja saṁvārī piya ghara āye
hilamila mangala gāyau |
mīrā ke prabhu hari abhināsī
bhāga bhalo jina pāyau ||

> O clouds, bring rain
> and pour
> in tiny drops:
> the wind's refrain

becomes a roar;
the cuckoo calls,
the clouds spread
on the sky as a dark pall.
      I have made the bed
      for my Beloved,
      come, friends, sing
      for the Lord Deathless;
      he indeed is blessed
      who can attain him.

68. *mehā barasavo kare re,*
    āja to ramiyo mere ghara re |
    nahīṁ būṁda megha ghana barasai,
    sūkhe saravara bhara re |
    bahuta dinā pai pītama pāyo,
    bichurana ko mohi ḍara re |
    mīrā kahai ati neha jurāyo,
    maiṁ liyo purabalo vara re ||

    It is raining
    let it,
    what do I care?
    my Lover is here with me.
        O rain! you may flood the dried ponds
        with your tiny drops,
        what do I care?
        my Lover is with me
        today:
        he has come after long,
        but I fear he may go away.
    Our love is strong
    for in a previous life
    we were
    husband and wife.[77]

69. *kaise jiūṁ rī māī*
    hari bina kaise jiyūṁ rī |
    udaka dādura pīnavata hai,
    jala meṁ upajāi |
    pala eka jala kūṁ mīna bisarae

talaphata mara jāī |
piyā bina pīlī bhaī re,
jyaum kāṭha ghuna khāya
auṣadha mūla na sancarai re,
bālā baida phiri jaya |
udāsī hoya bana bana phirūm re,
bithā tana chāī |
dāsī mīrā lāla giradhara
milyau hai sukhadāī ||

> Without my Beloved
> I can't keep
> alive,
> can the frog exist
> of rain
> deprived?
> water-starved,
> can the fish even a moment
> survive?
>> When Kṛṣṇa is away
>> I waste in sorrow,
>> as by wormwood's made
>> the wood hollow.
> No drug can cure me
> no physician heal,
> I wander in the woods
> wild with grief.
>> Giradhara is my Lover,
>> Lord of my life,
>> only his coming
>> can bring me delight.

70. *lagana hamārī syāma sūm lāgī,*
    nainā nirakha sukha pāya |
    sājām simgāra suhānām sajanī,
    prītama milyām dhāya |
    baraṇā baryām bāpuro
    janamyā janama nasāya |
    baryām sājana sāmvaro rī,
    mhāro curalo amara ho jāya |
    janama janama ro kāṇhaḍo,

mhāri prīta bujhāya |
mīrā re prabhu hari abināsī,
kaba re milasyo āya ||

> *What Mīrā said to her companion*
> Possessed
> by Kṛṣṇa's love
> I adorned myself
> to entice him,
> for now my eyes
> delight in
> him alone, my friend:
> and he came to meet
> me on swift feet.
>> Friend, the marriage bond
>> lasts only as long
>> as one's husband lives;
>> therefore I have pledged
>> myself to Kṛṣṇa and wed
>> him who'll ever be mine,
>> the Lord deathless.
> In previous lives, O Giradhara,
> you and I were one,
> I am waiting, Lover,
> O when will you come?

71. *bande bandagī mata bhūla |*
cāra dinā kī kara le khūbī,
jyum̐ dāḍima madā phūla |
āyā thā e lobha ke kāraṇa,
mūla gamāyā bhūla |
mīrā ke prabhu giradhara nāgara
rahanā hai be hajūra ||

> Do not forget
> to adore the Lord
> do not forget.
>> Life is short,
>> do good to others while yet
>> there's time; or like
>> the pomegranate flower

                    your glory will be shed.
          And you'll regret
          that you did not do
          all that you should have done.
                    Remember that for you,
                    as for everyone,
                    there's death.

72. *prabhu so milana kaise hoya |*
     pāṁca pahara dhandhe meṁ bīte,
     tīna pahara rahe soya |
     mānasa janama amolaka pāyo,
     sotaiṁ ḍaryo khoya |
     mīrā ke prabhu giradhara bhajīye
     honī hoya so hoya ||

          O deluded man
          how can you attain God
          when out of eight *paharas*[78]
          you spend five in household tasks
          and three in sleep?
                    When thus you while away
                    your precious life
                    then say,
          how can God be
          within your reach?
          Therefore chant the name of Giradhara
          with your mind carefree,
          desire not the fruit, only work,
          and let what will be, be.

73. *letāṁ letāṁ rāma nāma re,*
     lokariāṁ to lājāṁ mare chai |
     hari mandira jātāṁ pāvaliyā re dūkhe,
     phira āve sāro gāma re |
     jhagaro thāya tyāṁ dauṛī jāya re
     mukī ne ghara nā kāma re |
     bhāṁḍa bhavaiyā gaṇikā nṛta karatāṁ,
     besī rahe cāroṁ jāma re |
     mīrā ke prabhu giradhara nāgara,
     caraṇa kamala cita hāma re ||

Men stuck in the world's mire
are ashamed
to take God's name.
    Their feet tire
    in going to temples
    yet they delight
    to walk miles and miles
    in their village:
and if there's a fight
they'll leave their work
and be there in a minute!
    if there's a nautch
    of prostitutes or dancing girls
    somewhere
    they'll sit engrossed
    all the *paharas*
    there.[79]
My Lord is Giradhara
it's him alone I seek,
and my heart yearns ever
for his lotus-feet.

74. *rī mere pāra nikasa gayā,*
sāṁvare māryā tīra |
biraha anala lagī ura antari,
vyākula bhayā sarīra |
ita uta cita cālai kabahūṁ nahi
ḍārī prema janjīra |
ke jāne mero prītama pyāro
aura na jāne pīra |
kahā kahūṁ mere basa nahiṁ sajanī
naina jharata doū nīra |
mīrā kahai prabhu tuma miliyā bina
praṇa dharata nahiṁ dhīra ||

    What Mīrā said to her companion
    My heart, friend, aches
    for my Lord,
    as though rent
    by a deadly dart.

Parting's fire
burns and pains,
where shall I go
I'm bound with love's chain.
Only my dear Beloved
can know
my agony,
only he:
tears rise in my eyes
and flow
endlessly.
  Bereft of you, Kṛṣṇa,
  my grieved heart
  knows no peace.

75. *mhāre ḍere ājyo jī maharāja |*
cuna cuna kaliyāṁ seja bichāyo,
nakhasikha paharyo sāja |
janama janama dāsī terī,
tuma mere siratāja |
mīrā ke prabhu hari abināsī,
darasaṇa dījyo āja ||

Come home, Lover
I have gathered
the choicest buds
to make your bed;
I've adorned myself
to please you
  I'm your slave
  through many lives,
  O Master, O Lord deathless
  I await you
  with bated breath.

76. *tuma bina merī kauna khabara le*
gobaradhana giradharī |
mora mukuṭa pītāmbara śobhāṁ,
kuṇḍala rī chaba nyārī |
bharī sabhā mā drupada sutāṁ rī,
rakhyā lāja murārī |

mīrā ke prabhu giradhara nāgara,
caraṇa kaṁvala balihārī ||

> Who's my refuge
> save you, Kṛṣṇa?—
> in yellow silk dressed
> your earrings glittering
> a crown of peacock-feathers
> adorning your head.
>> You save Draupadī[80]
>> from dishonour
>> in the assembly-hall,
>> but at me
>> you do not glance at all.[81]
> Giradhara is my Lord
> to whom my life is pledged,
> on his lotus-feet
> I've cast myself.

77. *cālaṁ agama vā desa,*
kāla dekhyāṁ ḍarāṁ |
bharāṁ prema rū hoya
hansa kelyāṁ karāṁ |
sadhā santa ro saṅga
jñāna jugatāṁ karāṁ |
dharāma sāṁvaro dhyāno
citta ujalo karāṁ |
sīla ghūṁgharā bāṁdha
tosa niratā karāṁ |
sājāṁ sola siṅgara,
soṇāro rākhaḍāṁ |
sāṁvaliyā sūṁ prīta,
aurāṁ sūṁ ākhaḍāṁ ||

> Come to that land, O Mind,
> where Death fears to go,
> where in the pools of Love
> Souls delight to sport,
> there live holy men
> from whom wisdom flows;
> there, O mind, you'll chant Kṛṣṇa's name

and be made pure.
In that land 'twere as though
Virtue dances with jingle-bells
in each jingle of which
Contentment dwells.
There women adorn themselves
with the sixteen adornments[82]
and wear bangles of gold
to entice their sweethearts;
there Kṛṣṇa is adored, O Mind,
more than other gods.

78. *lāgī sohī jānai,*
    kaṭhana lagana dī pira |
    vipati paḍyaṁ koī nikaṭa na āvai,
    sukha meṁ sabakī sīra |
    bāhari ghāva kachu nahiṁ dīsai,
    roma roma dī pīra |
    jana mīrā giradhara ke ūpara |
    sadakai karūṁ sarīra ||

    Only he who has loved
    can know love's distress;
    in palmy days men flock
    in grief he's by himself.
        Love's agony is like
        a wound that looks all right
        but pains through every limb
        for the pain is deep inside.
    My Beloved is Kṛṣṇa,
    says Mīrā, and to him
    I've surrendered my life.

79. *ṇāto sāṁvaro rī mhāsū,*
    tanaka na toḍyāṁ jāya |
    pānāṁ jyūṁ pīlī paṛi rī,
    loga kahyāṁ piṇḍavāya |
    bābala vada bulāiyā rī,
    mhāṁrī bāhaṁ dikhāya |
    baidā marama na jāṇā rī,
    mhāṁrī hivaṛo karakāṁ jāya |

mīrā vyākula virahani rī,
prabhu darasana dīnyo āya ||

 What Mīrā said to her companion
 My love for Kṛṣṇa is deep
 it can never cease to be;
  like a withered leaf
  grief has made me yellow
  but my people feel
  jaundice makes me so!
 They called a physician
 who felt my pulse
 and to relieve me
 he gave me drugs;
 but what can drugs do
 when the sickness is love?
  Friend, parting's fire makes
  my heart burn,
  it seems it will break
  if Kṛṣṇa does not come.
 Hasten, O Lover,
 for I know no peace,
 only your coming
 can end my grief.

80. *rī mahāṁ baiṭhyā jāgāṁ,*
 jagata saba sovāṁ |
 virahana baiṭhyāṁ rangamahala māṁ,
 nena laḍyā povāṁ |
 ika virahani hama aisī dekhī,
 aṁsuvana kī mālā povai |
 tārāṁ ganatāṁ rena bihānāṁ
 mukha ghariyārī jovāṁ |
 mīrā re prabhu giradhara nāgara
 mila bichaḍyā nā hovāṁ ||

 While all the world slept
 I could not sleep;
 I saw in a palace room[83]
 where lovers meet,
 a girl afflicted

with parting's grief.
    She and her lover
    gazed at each other,
    but their love did not blossom I fear,
    for forlorn
    she sat alone
    stringing a garland of tears.
She would keep waking
counting the stars,
ever waiting
for her sweetheart.
    Is it fair
    O Giradhara, say,
    after meeting me,
    so to keep away?

81. *yahi vidhi bhakti kaise hoya |*
    mana kī maila hiye se na chūṭī
    diyo tilaka sira dhoya |
    kāma kūkara lobha ḍorī
    bāṁdhi mohiṁ caṇḍāla |
    krodha kasāī rahata ghaṭa meṁ
    kaise mileṁ gopāla |
    bilāra viṣayā lālacī re,
    tāhi bhojana deta |
    dīna hīna hvai kṣudhā tarasai,
    rāma nāma na leta |
    āpa hī āpa pujāya kai re,
    phūle anga na samāta |
    abhimāna ṭilā kie bahu,
    kahu jala kahāṁ ṭhaharāta |
    jā tere hiye antara kī jāṇe
    tāsoṁ kapaṭa na banai |
    hirade hari ko nāṁva na āve,
    mukha te maṇiyā gaṇaī |
    hari hitu soṁ heta kara,
    saṁsāra āsā tyāga |
    dāsī mīrā lāla giradhara,
    sahaja kara bairāga ||

How can devotion
ever come to you, say,
if your mind's sunk in
evil always?
> What if you bathe
> and put on a *tilaka* mark;[84]
> if craving still sways you
> as a filth-eating dog
> and butcher-like violence and rage
> waylay you,
> how can you ever reach God?
If greed for sense-pleasures
like a preying cat
invades your mind,
and at that
you feed it,
it will remain.
Though with hunger and thirst
sorely taxed,
yet you'll not chant Rāma's name.
> You have built dams
> of vanity all around you,
> how can the waters of devotion
> ever come through?
God can see
what's in your heart
you cannot deceive him;
O deluded man, remember,
only devotion can please him.
> You absently tell the beads
> your mind elsewhere;
> do you think the All-knowing
> will heed such prayer?
O man,
befriend
God's devotees,
do not put your trust in
men.
> Mīrā says, O Kṛṣṇa,
> I'm your slave,

show me the way to
renunciation.

REFERENCES

1. Hindus believe that if one dies in Kāśī (modern Varanasi) he will get *mokṣa* (emancipation). The word *karavata* means 'a saw', thus signifying death. It was believed to be a saw by which if a man cut his neck he would attain heaven.

2. Some commentators have taken *cahara* to mean 'a bird', but this doesn't seem likely. So it has been taken to mean *causara* = 'dice', and *bājī* 'a throw (of dice)'

3. A *tilaka* is an ornamental mark made by red powder or paste on the middle of the forehead.

4. Braja-maids are *gopīs* or cowherd girls associated with Kṛṣṇa.

5. Giradhārī (from *giri* = 'a hill' and *dhāraṇa* = 'holding'), is one of Kṛṣṇa's names. According to legend the boy Kṛṣṇa persuaded the people of Gokul to cease offering prayers to Indra, heaven's king. The enraged Indra caused a heavy downpour for many days. But Kṛṣṇa held the Goverdhana mount on his little finger and saved the people from drowning by sheltering them under it.

6. Kāma is the Hindu god of Love (Eros, Cupid). He is the lord of the *apsarasas* or heavenly nymphs. He is shown as holding a bow of sugarcane, the bowstring a line of bees. Each arrow of his is tipped with a distinct flower. He is represented as a handsome youth riding on a parrot and attended by nymphs, one of whom holds his banner having a fish on a red ground.

7. Kṛṣṇa is called *tribhaṅgī* (*tri* = 'three'; *bhaṅgī* = 'waves'), because he is often seen standing in three undulations, the flute on which he plays held aslant against his lips. In his *Satasaī* the poet Bihārī speaks of this form in a rather amusing manner: 'I will not leave my crookedness, Kṛṣṇa, even though people may reproach me, for if I remain straight you, with your form of triple undulations, will have trouble dwelling in me!'

8. The *cakora* is the Indian rock or sand partridge (*Caccabis chukor*). According to traditional Hindi poetry, the bird subsists only on the nectar it derives from the moonbeams.

9. Balarāma, Kṛṣṇa's elder brother, is regarded as one of Viṣṇu's incarnations. It is told in the *Mahābhārata* that Viṣṇu took two hairs, one white and the other black, and so Balarāma was fair and Kṛṣṇa dark. Both of them were brought up by their foster parents at Gokula. That's why they are mentioned together here, wandering on the Yamunā bank, where Kṛṣṇa sported with the cowherd maids of Vṛndāvana.

10. *Pacaraṁga colā—pāñca* = 'five'; *raṁga* = 'colour'; *colā* = 'robe', i.e., a robe of five colours. Some commentators take this to mean 'the human body made of the five constituents, namely, air, water, fire, earth and ether', as the *Rāmacaritmānasa* of Tulsīdāsa says: *chita jala pāvaka gagana samīra, pañca racita ati adhama sarīrā,* 'this greatly wretched body is formed of the five elements, namely, earth, water, fire, ether and air' (Kiṣkindhā Kāṇḍa, 10.1). Thus these commentators give a philosophical twist to these words. But it doesn't seem likely that Mīrā meant that, for her emphasis here is on love, not philosophy. So the simpler interpretation of a robe of five colours has been taken in the rendering. A *colā*, strictly speaking, is a robe worn by ascetics, so here the surrender of her body to Kṛṣṇa does not imply lovemaking, but a spiritual union.

11. *Jhiramiṭa*—This is a kind of game in which one hides himself or herself behind

a veil and then after a minute or so removes it. Thus it is a kind of hide-and-seek.

12. Hari is another name for Viṣṇu, whose incarnation Kṛṣṇa was.

13. Prahlāda was a *daitya* and son of Hiraṇyakaśipu. Hiraṇyakaśipu had ousted Indra and become heaven's king. Prahlāda was a devotee of Kṛṣṇa. This enraged his father, who sought to kill him in many ways, but Kṛṣṇa protected him and at last killed Hiraṇyakaśipu by incarnating himself as Narasimha (the Man-lion). According to the *Padma Purāṇa*, Prahlāda was raised to the position of Indra.

14. Dhruva is the pole star. The *Viṣṇu Purāṇa* records that Manu Swāyambhuva had two sons, Priyavrata and Uttarapāda. The latter son had two wives. Dhruva was the son of one of them, but the other was Uttarapāda's favourite wife, and she ill-treated Dhruva. Dhruva, however, remained submissive, and finally left home and became a *ṛṣi* and performed stern austerities, thus winning Viṣṇu's favour. Viṣṇu raised him to the sky as the pole star.

15. Kāliā *nāga* (*nāga* = 'a serpent') was a deadly serpent with five heads living on the bed of the Yamunā river. His mouths emitted fire and smoke and laid waste the country of Gokula where the boy Kṛṣṇa lived. Kṛṣṇa dived into the river and overcame the serpent, but spared its life on condition that he left the Yamunā and went away to the ocean. To celebrate his victory Kṛṣṇa danced on the subdued Kāliā's heads.

16. Ahalyā, daughter of Brahmā, married the sage, Gautama. She was very beautiful, so much so that Indra, the king of heaven was infatuated with her. One day when Gautama had left his hermitage for his ritual prayers, Indra assumed the sage's form and went in to make love to her. She allowed him to, thinking that it was her husband returned from prayers. It so happened that just as he was coming out after ravishing Ahalyā, the sage returned. When he saw his double before him, he used his power of divination and knew it was Indra. He cursed Indra to remain impotent and his wife to become a block of stone, and await the coming of Rāma, who would revive her. When Rāma was in the forest in the period of his exile, he touched the stone with his foot and Ahalyā came to life and went away to heaven.

17. The cowherd girls of Vṛndāvana (*gopīs*) with whom Kṛṣṇa sported.

18. For lifting the Goverdhana mount, see fn, to verse 4.

19. That is, 'save me from further rebirths and give me emancipation.'

20. The *cātaka* (or *papīhā*)—(*Cuculus melanoleucos*) is the pied-crested cuckoo. According to traditional Indian fable, which Hindi poets often refer to, the bird is believed to drink only the raindrops falling in October, the month in which rainfall is very rare. Hindi poets take this to symbolize devotion. Its call is also very plaintive.

21. Some commentators feel that this depicts the Vedāntic concept of the identity of the Soul (*ātman*) and the World Soul (*Brahman*). But it seems the lines are only an expression of Mīrā's rhapsody and an expression of her love for Kṛṣṇa, rather than a pointer to the Advaita philosophy of the monists.

22. Sāvana is the fifth month of the Hindu year, corresponding to July-August. It heralds the rainy season and is therefore very delightful after the blistering heat of the Indian summer.

23. *Tulasī* (sometimes identified with the basil plant), is considered sacred by Hindus. Its leaves are offered to idols worshipped by them. So it is invariably found in Hindu homes, particularly of the devout, and grown in pots or in the ground and in courtyards.

24. Both Western writers and Indian poets like Jayadeva, Vidyāpati, Keśavadāsa and so forth, not understanding Rādhā's significance, have misrepresented her as a flirt who is made love to by Kṛṣṇa. In truth she is said ⁿ₂ be the incarnation of Lakṣmī, the consort of Lord Viṣṇu. She represents, metaphorically, the Soul drawn to the Divine. So the sense here is that the Soul, hearing the call of the Divine, goes about seeking it.

25. Rāma, one of Viṣṇu's incarnation, is the most popularly worshipped of the Hindu gods. Professor Williams says: 'the Rāma legends have always retained their purity, and unlike those of Brahmā, Kṛṣṇa, Śiva and Durgā, have never been mixed up with indecencies and licentiousness.' 'Rāma! Rāma!' is a common form of salutation. Though primarily Mīrā's verses address Kṛṣṇa, a few are in adoration of Rāma.

26. For Rādhā see fn, to verse 14 ante.

27. The three worlds are heaven, earth and the nether world.

28. Hari is Viṣṇu, here the word stands for Kṛṣṇa who is believed to be Viṣṇu's incarnation.

29. The idea is that Mīrā will dance before Kṛṣṇa to captivate him. If she succeeds and awakens love in his heart, she'll know that her old love for him from lives past was true.

30. *Sanjīvanī būṭī* (*būṭī* = 'herb') is believed to be a herb growing on the Himalaya mountains by administering which in time, life can be revived if extinct. It was brought by Hanumān the god Māruti, for Lakṣmaṇa, Rāma's brother when Rāvaṇa's son had hurled a celestial weapon at him.

31. The reference is to the finely made and costly dresses of Vijayanagara in Southern India (*dikhaṇī* or *dakṣiṇa* means 'South' and *cīra* means 'cloth').

32. This isn't quite the concept now, but Mīrā is speaking of her own times. It is the orthodox view and not confined to the Hindu ethos alone, either. Did not Milton say 'He for God only, she for God in him?'

33. The word in the text is *makara*, which can be taken to mean an alligator or the tenth sign of the Zodiac. It would hardly make any sense to say that the fishes have left the pond to meet the alligator. The line has therefore been interpreted as follows: The fish which represents the sign of Pisces in the Zodiac and which is on its top part, has come down to meet the crocodile which represents the sign of the Zodiac placed halfway down. Kṛṣṇa's earrings dangle on his cheeks. Thus the earring which is perhaps fish-shaped, represents Pisces, and his cheeks the House of Capricorn. However, the comparison seems to be far-fetched.

34. This is one of those verses in which Mīrā mentions Rāma along with Kṛṣṇa. Both of them are believed to be Viṣṇu's incarnations. So it is all the same whether she addresses the one or the other.

35. The word in the text is *toraṇa* which could mean a welcome gateway with festoons. But the more likely sense is that the marriage-pavilion was decked with festoons, as is usual in Hindu marriage ceremonies.

36. A *ṭīkā* is an ornamental mark made on the middle of the brow. Lamp-black is applied to the inner part of the eyelids to make the eyes look dark and lovely.

37. Bhīls are a wild mountain-tribe dwelling on the banks of the Narmada river. A bhīlanī is such a tribal woman. The reference is to Śabarī, a low-caste tribal woman who, however, was an unswerving devotee of Rāma (Viṣṇu's incarnation). She welcomed him when he went to her hut in the forest, during the course of his exile. She had only wild plums to offer him to eat. In her extreme

love for Rāma, she bit off a portion of each plum, discarding the sour ones, and offering the sweet ones, unmindful of the fact that she had tasted them herself! Rāma, however, ate them all lovingly and without any hesitation. The incident is mentioned in the *Rāmāyaṇa*.

38. *Gopī* means a cowherd girl. It is mentioned in the *Bhāgavata Purāṇa* that Kṛṣṇa sported with them on the banks of the Yamunā river. They are believed to be sages who aspired for emancipation and to achieve it, were born as *gopīs*.

39. Mīrā was very sore about the apathy of the Rāṇās towards sadhus and holy men. She was also censorious of their (the Rāṇās') profligate living. This could be a reflection of her life's experience.

40. The *gopīs* of Braja carried earthen pots containing butter and curd to sell. The boy Kṛṣṇa is believed to have a great liking for both butter and curd.

41. For *papīhā* (or *cātaka*) see fn, to verse 11.

42. Indra is the Hindu god of the firmament and the deity of the atmosphere. The idea appears to be that the earth becomes green again when the rains come. So symbolically it prepares to meet Indra, who is the giver of the rain. See also fn, to verse 4.

43. For *papīhā* see fn, to verse 11. The word *pī* or *piā* means 'beloved'. So Mīrā imagines that the bird (calling *pī, pī*) is really calling out to its mate, the female bird, and that reminds her of her Lover, Kṛṣṇa.

44. Sāvana is the month of greatest rainfall in India. See fn, to verse 13.

45. The text says *karma*, which means 'works'. The law of karma, which is a salient feature of Hinduism (and also of Buddhism), implies that one gets rewarded for good works done and punished for the evil ones. Hindus believe in rebirth. So the deeds done in one life, have their effect on future lives too. However, the emphasis here is on destiny not karma, otherwise why should a truthful king or a virtuous queen get punishment? The idea is that the law of destiny is mysterious and inexorable (cf., verse 35). Hence karma has been taken to imply destiny here.

46. Hariścandra was the twenty-eighth king of the Solar race and son of Triśaṅku. He was celebrated for his piety, justice and truthfulness. According to the *Mārkaṇḍeya Purāṇa* the sage Viśvāmitra was practising austerities to master the Sciences. The Sciences, represented by a woman, cried out in lamentation. The merciful king, Hariścandra went to aid them. This enraged the sage, who, demanding his right as a brahmin to obtain as sacrifice whatever he wanted, asked the king to hand over all his wealth and kingdom, his wife and his child. Hariścandra became a destitute and had to take up service with a Ḍoma (a man of a low-caste), who made him work at the cremation ground, where he had to draw water from the well for the ablution of those who went to cremate the corpse. He was duty-bound to take part of the cloth covering the corpses. It so happened that Hariścandra's son died of snake-bite and his wife, in tatters, came to cremate him. Hariścandra stuck to the condition imposed, and demanded the usual part of the cloth from her too. Full of grief, his wife and he decided to immolate themselves on the funeral pyre of their son. But instantly the gods arrived. It was all a kind of test, and the king's son, wife, wealth and kingdom were restored to him. Though the end was happy, Hariścandra had to undergo immense suffering and humiliation.

47. After the Mahābhārata war, the Pāṇḍavas (Arjuna, Bhīma, Yudhiṣṭhira, Nakula and Sahadeva) accompanied by their mother, Kuntī and their wife Draupadī (she was married to all the Pāṇḍava brothers), left their kingdom and went

away to the Himalaya mountains, where they died one by one, except Yudhiṣṭhira who was taken to heaven on Indra's *vimāna* (air-chariot). Draupadī was the first to die.

48. Bali was a good and virtuous *daitya* (demon) king. Through his devotion and austerities he humbled Indra by aspiring to replace him, and also took possession of the three worlds. The gods appealed to Viṣṇu who took the form of a dwarf (the Vāmana or Dwarf avatar). He went to Bali and asked as a boon just three steps of land. Unsuspecting, Bali readily agreed. The Dwarf stepped over heaven and earth in two strides, but due to Bali's goodness and Bali's grandson, Prahlāda, who was a Viṣṇu-devotee, he left him the nether regions (*pātāla*). A *yajña* is a religious sacrifice. Bali carried it out to achieve a certain objective.

49. The reference is to Mīrā's brother-in-law who sent her a cup of poison ordering her to drink it, so that he may be rid of her. She drank the poison, which by Kṛṣṇa's grace was instantly turned to nectar.

50. The verse is about Vikramājīta, the Rāṇā (ruler) of Mewāra, and Mīrā's brother-in-law. His family was of the Sisodiā clan—hence the word *sisodiā*.

51. Kṛṣṇa was born at Mathura. His mother was Devakī and his father Vasudeva. Devakī's cousin, Kaṁsa had usurped the throne and proved to be a cruel tyrant. Nārada, the celestial sage, had foretold that one of Devakī's sons would kill him. So he destroyed all her sons as soon as they were born. However, Kṛṣṇa was miraculously taken to Gokula, where he was brought up by his foster-parents, Nanda and Yaśodā. Gokula was the scene of his sports with Rādhā and the *gopīs*. Later he moved to Mathura to slay Kaṁsa, free his parents from prison where they had been kept by him (Kaṁsa) and restore the throne to Ugrasena, the rightful ruler. Here Mīrā bemoans Kṛṣṇa's departure to Mathura.

52. *Duija* is the second day of the lunar fortnight. The moon is seen for a very short time on *duija* night. So when one wishes to say 'You are rarely seen these days', this is idiomatically expressed in Hindi by 'You have become like the moon on *duija* night.'

53. For *cātaka* also called *papīhā* see fn, to verse 11.

54. The Tīja is a Hindu festival celebrated by women.

55. *Phāga* is a song sung in the Holī festival, which usually falls in March.

56. Basanta-pañcamī is the end of the severe winter season, and the beginning of spring.

57. The Holī festival is usually celebrated in March. After bonfires are burnt, revellers sprinkle coloured water or coloured powders on one another. After midday they dress up and go round meeting friends and relations.

58. It is a superstitious belief among Hindus that the cawing of a crow at one's door, signifies someone's arrival. That's why the crows' cawing fill her with hope of Kṛṣṇa's coming.

59. There are six *ṛtus* in the Hindu calendar. Each *ṛtu* (season) comprising two months. These are Vasanta or Madhuṛtu (spring)—March to April; Grīṣma (summer)—May to June; Varṣā (the rainy season)—July to August; Śarada (autumn)—September to October; Hemanta (winter)—November to December; and Śiśira (the cool season)—January to February. The months according to the Hindu calendar are: (1) Caita or Caitra (March-April); (2) Baisākha (April-May); (3) Jeṣṭha or Jeṭha (May-June); (4) Asāṛha (June-July); (5) Sāvana (July-August); (6) Bhādoṁ (August-September); (7) Kuār (September-October); (8) Kārtika (October-November); (9) Aghana (November-December); (10) Pausa or Pūṣa (December-January); (11) Māgha (January-February); and (12) Phāguna

(February-March).

60. For the significance of death in Kāśī *(karavata kāsī)*, see fn, to verse 2.

61. For *cataka* see fn, to verse 11. The rain which the *cātaka* drinks is called the Svāti rain because it falls in the period when the moon is in the fifteenth asterism (*svāti*—'the fifteenth asterism'). Since the bird is believed to drink only the Svāti rain-drops, which fall in winter when, in India, few clouds bear rain, the poetess says she is as restless for Krṣṇa as the *cātaka* for the Svāti rain-drops.

62. The Rāṇā refers to Vikramājīta, Mīrā's brother-in-law.

63. Hindus believe that it is only after eighty-four lakh (8,400,000) lives on earth, birth as a human being is obtained. What Mīrā means is that one who leads an evil life will be reborn in some lower form of existence as for example, beasts, birds and so forth. Thereafter the soul will be able to get a human body only after going through eighty-four lakh lives. In the *Bhagavadgītā* Krṣṇa says that he casts evil persons in lower wombs: *kṣipāmi ajastram aśubhāna āsurīṣu eva yoniṣu* (16.19). In his *Crest Jewel of Wisdom* Śaṅkarācārya says that birth as a man is obtained with great difficulty.

64. *Mokṣa* or *mukti* is believed to be that state in which the Soul *(ātmā)* unites with the Cosmic Absolute *(Brahman)*. This state is difficult to attain, for it is got by continued striving for God life after life. Nonetheless it is the sole objective of human endeavour. Aldous Huxley says, 'Man's life on earth has only one end and purpose, to identify himself with the eternal Self and so to come to unitive knowledge of the Divine Ground.'

65. In some recensions as those of Krishnadeva Sharma and Padmavati, the word in the first line is *jharī* not *ḍarī*. We have followed the anthology of Chunnilal Śeṣa in this verse, where it is *ḍarī*.

66. For *mokṣa* see fn, to verse 53.

67. The text says 'Rāma' *(he rāmā)*, but Mīrā was a Kṛṣṇa devotee, even though she sometimes speaks about Rāma in her verses. Besides, the rest of the *pada* fits in with Krṣṇa. So Krṣṇa has been substituted for Rāma. As both are incarnations of Viṣṇu, it is really all the same.

68. Giradhara is another name for Krṣṇa. See fn, to verse 9.

69. According to the Purāṇas the Viyadgangā or the heavenly Gangā flowed from the toe of Viṣṇu. It had to be brought down to the earth by the prayer of Bhagīratha (a descendant of Sagara) to purify the ashes of the sixty thousand sons of King Sagara who had been burned by the angry glance of the sage Kapila. It is therefore also called the Bhāgīrathī. Gangā was angry on having to leave the celestial regions, so Śiva had to take it on his matted hair to save the earth from the shock of its fall. Hence the Gangā is also known as Hara-śekhara or 'crest of Śiva'.

70. The three worlds are the earth, heavens and the nether regions. The subterranean Sarasvatī is believed to have existed along with the sacred Gangā, and at some time flowed up to the ocean as the Gangā does.

71. When Rāma was banished because of the intrigue of Kaikeyī, his step-mother, Bharata, her son, went to the forest where Rāma was living as a hermit, to persuade him to come back and assume the crown of Ayodhyā. Rāma was unwilling, as this would mean breaking his father's word. So Bharata took Rāma's sandal, and reverentially placing them on his head, took them to Ayodhyā and placing them on a platform worshipped them every morning before taking up matters of state, as Rāma's regent.

72. Kevaṭa was the boatman who took Rāma across the river Saryū while Rāma was

in the exile period. He wanted to wash Rāma's feet as he was a Rāma-devotee. The sage Gautama had cursed his wife Ahalyā to be turned into stone. Rāma's touch revived her and she flew away to heaven (see fn, to verse 9). So Kevaṭa gave this excuse for washing Rāma's feet.

73. While in the forest, Lakṣmaṇa, Rāma's brother, cut off the nose of Sūrpaṇakhā, the demon-king Rāvaṇa's sister. In order to avenge her, Rāvaṇa prevailed on Mārīca, his nephew, to take the form of a golden deer, so that Rāma should chase it to shoot it and get the skin for Sītā. Then Rāvaṇa would go and carry Sītā away. The plan worked, and Rāvaṇa took Sītā away on his *vimāna* (air-chariot). The idea expressed is that even while being the All-knower, Rāma played a part in consonance with the avatar in which he assumed the human form with a certain purpose.

74. Rāma met Sugrīva while he was wandering in the forest during his exile. He learnt that Bāli, his brother, had usurped his kingdom and also forcibly abducted his wife. Rāma promised to help Sugrīva. He killed Bāli and restored his kingdom. In return Sugrīva was of great help in the search for Sītā and there after in assisting Rāma in the war with Rāvaṇa, who had carried Sītā away to his kingdom, Lankā.

75. Vibhīṣaṇa was Rāvaṇa's brother. But he was a devout demon and a Rāma-devotee. He counselled Rāvaṇa to make peace with Rāma and return Sītā. Rāvaṇa got enraged at this and kicked Vibhīṣaṇa and insulted him before all those assembled in his court. So Vibhīṣaṇa went over to Rāma, who accepted him.

   All these incidents are mentioned in Tulsī's *Rāmāyaṇa (Rāmacaritmānasa)*. Though Mīrā was a Kṛṣṇa-devotee, she occasionally addressed Rāma in her *padas*.

76. The reference is to the brother-in-law of Mīrā, Rāṇā Vikramājīta of Mewāra.

77. A *sāligarāma* or *śalagrāma* is an idol of Lord Viṣṇu in of the shape of a smooth black stone.

78. Mīrā loved Kṛṣṇa in the *mādhurya* way of Vaiṣṇava devotion which is expressed metaphorically in a husband-wife kind of relationship. The sense is not to be taken literally.

79. A *pahara* is a period of three hours. Thus there are eight *paharas* in a day and night.

80. For *paharas* see fn, to verse 79 ante. Four *paharas* means twelve hours.

81. Draupadī was the wife of the five Pāṇḍavas (all brothers). She was staked and lost to the Kauravas in a game of dice. Duḥśāsana, one of the Kauravas, tried to disrobe her in the assembly-hall. Kṛṣṇa came to her aid, and the more he pulled her sari the more it grew in length, till he (Duḥśāsana) fell exhausted on the floor.

82. Poet Keśavadāsa gives details of the sixteen adornments: (1) ablutions like cleaning the teeth and the body; (2) bathing; (3) wearing spotlessly clean clothes; (4) braiding the hair; (5) applying cosmetics of sandalwood paste etc.; (6) putting vermilion in the parting of the hair; (7) painting a crescent of sandalwood paste on the forehead; (8) painting a black mole on the cheek; (9) anointing the limbs with saffron; (10) staining the palms with the red dye of myrtle leaves; (11) chewing betel leaves; (12) chewing cardamom (both of these to sweeten the breath); (13) wearing gold ornaments; (14) putting on flower garlands; (15) applying black powder *(misi)* to the crevices of the teeth to make the teeth shine out the more; and (16) applying collyrium (lamp-black) to the inner eyelids to make the eyes attractive.

83. A *raṅgamahala* is a room in a palace set apart for the entertainment of chief-

tains and rulers, who spent quite a bit of their time in sensual pleasures like drinking, song and dance. The 'girl' is, of course Mīrā herself, and speaking about her is only a way to express her own longing for Kṛṣṇa.

84. The *tilaka* mark implies here a sacerdotal mark put on the middle of the forehead, vertical or horizontal, according to the sect to which the Hindu belongs.

Bibliography

ENGLISH

Basu, A.N., *Mira Bai, Her Life and Songs,* Shantiniketan, 1929.

Farquhar, J.N., *An Outline of Religious Literature in India,* Oxford, 1920; rep., Delhi, 1967.

Grierson, G.A., *The Modern Vernacular Literature of Hindustan,* Calcutta, 1889.

Keay, F.E., *A History of Hindi Literature,* Calcutta, 1960.

Mehta, S.S., *Mira Bai, Saint of Mewad,* Bombay, n.d.

Oman, J.C., *The Mystics, Ascetics and Saints of India: A Study in Sadhuism,* London, 1903; rep., Delhi, 1972.

Sarda, H.B., *Maharana Sanga the Hindupat, the First Great Leader of the Rajput Race,* New Delhi, 1970.

Sitaram, Lala, *Selections from Hindi Literature.*

Tandon, R.C., *Songs of Mira Bai.*

Taraporevala, I.J. Sorabji, *Selections from Classical Gujarati Literature.*

Tod, J., *Annals and Antiquities of Rajasthan,* 2 vols., London, 1829-30; rep., New Delhi, 1982.

Tripathi, G.M., *The Classical Poets of Gujarat and their Influence on Society and Morals,* Bombay, 1958.

Vaswani, T.L., *Saint Mira,* Poona.

HINDI

Dhruvadasa, *Bhakta Nāmāvalī.*

Kayastha, Sundaradasa, *Mīrā Bāī kī Vandanā.*

Nabhadasa, *Bhaktamālā.*

Priyadasa, *Bhakti-rasa-bodhinī.*

Sharan, Siyarama, *Bhakti-sudha-bindu-svāda.*

Index